POETRY COMP

GREAT MINDS

Your World...Your Future...YOUR WORDS

From Wales Vol I
Edited by Kelly Oliver

First published in Great Britain in 2005 by:
Young Writers
Remus House
Coltsfoot Drive
Peterborough
PE2 9JX
Telephone: 01733 890066
Website: www.youngwriters.co.uk

All Rights Reserved

© *Copyright Contributors 2005*

SB ISBN 1 84602 081 6

Foreword

This year, the Young Writers' 'Great Minds' competition proudly presents a showcase of the best poetic talent selected from over 40,000 up-and-coming writers nationwide.

Young Writers was established in 1991 to promote the reading and writing of poetry within schools and to the youth of today. Our books nurture and inspire confidence in the ability of young writers and provide a snapshot of poems written in schools and at home by budding poets of the future.

The thought, effort, imagination and hard work put into each poem impressed us all and the task of selecting poems was a difficult but nevertheless enjoyable experience.

We hope you are as pleased as we are with the final selection and that you and your family continue to be entertained with *Great Minds From Wales Vol I* for many years to come.

Contents

Brecon High School, Powys
Joe Coleman (15)	1
Rhys Burgess (12)	2
Dafydd Maclennan (11)	2
David Jenkins (12)	3
Molly Owen (11)	3
Zoë Crane (15)	4
Ffion Miles (12)	5
Elin Rees (11)	6
Alwyn Lee (11)	6
Alun Davies (12)	7
Rhys Nicholls (11)	7
Emily Ham (13)	8
Dafydd Reeves (12)	9

St Michael's School, Dyfed
Hassan Izzat (13)	10
Harriet Clark (13)	11
Tom Townsend (13)	12
Stephanie Turner (13)	12
Greg Powles (13)	13
Kueni Victor Igbagiri (13)	14
Ruth Fletcher (13)	14
Lucy Jeffery (13)	15
Faaz Ashraf (13)	15
Lloyd Hopkin (13)	16
Amina Hussain (13)	16
Josephine Dingley (13)	17
Parvathy Vipulendran (13)	18
Ashley Eynon-Davies (13)	18
Sally Scourfield (13)	19
Kristian Hickin (13)	19
Rachel Llewellyn (13)	20
Barnaby Rees-Jones (13)	20
Matthew Watkins (13)	21
Tanu Verma (13)	22
James Prosser (13)	22
Shruti Uppala (13)	23
Waleed Khalik (14)	23

Viraj Ratnalikar (13)   24
Kristian Limpert (13)   25
Ryan Bowen (14)   26
Andrea Bertelli (13)   27
Atif Sabah (13)   28
Christopher Pavlou (13)   29
Sophie Adams (13)   30
Rhiân Hughes (14)   31
Bethany Sawyer (13)   32
Jessica Davies (13)   32
Lisa Tucker (13)   33
Nikita Poli (13)   33
Jenny Sze (13)   34

Sir Thomas Picton School, Haverfordwest

Owain Bladen (12)   34
Connor George (12)   35
Sam Parry (12)   35
George Davies (13)   36
Josh Balfe (14)   36
Laurie Williams (13)   37
Charlotte Butcher (12)   37
Natalie Richards (13)   38
Katy Evans (12)   38
Christina Morgan (12)   39
Poppy Purcell (12)   39
Laura Williams (12)   40
Luke Buntwal (13)   40
Rachel Davies (13)   41
Bryan Power (13)   42
Natasha Palmer (12)   42
Andrew Theobald (13)   43
Matthew Clark (13)   44
Kayleigh Turner (12)   44
Daisy Lewis (12)   45
Lindsay Collins (13)   46
Laura Venables (12)   46
Amy Rossiter (12)   47
Shreshta Musale (11)   47
Hannah Ainsworth (13)   48
Amy John (13)   48

Matthew Western (12)	49
Angharad Barnes (12)	50
Samuel Williams (11)	50
Holly Pretious (12)	51
Hannah Rolfe (12)	52
Chris Williams	52
Oliver Reyland (13)	53
Jordan Beavis (11)	53
Joshua Lee (12)	54
Sarah James (11)	54
Laura Hill (13)	55
James Riddiford (11)	55
Gavin Thomas (13)	56
Anastasia Pashen (11)	56
Kai Lumber (12)	57
Emma Tilley (14)	57
Cassey Bicknell (12)	58
Stewart Coombes (13)	59
Amy Davies (12)	60
Ben Clague (11)	60
Darren Johns (13)	61
Gareth Harries (13)	61
Alex Kirk (12)	62
Thomas Glover (12)	62
Christina Cunliffe (12)	63
Andrew Lamport (11)	63
Tania Hancock (12)	64
Jessie Jones (12)	65
Joanne Griffiths (12)	66
Sam Stayner (12)	66
Chris Chan (12)	67
Josey Protheroe (12)	67
Holly Richards (13)	68
Anthony Yau (12)	69
Robyn Fisher (13)	70
Curtis Elliott (13)	70
Danielle Jones (13)	71
Gareth Bateman (13)	72
Owain Glyn Evans (13)	73
Carl Rees (13)	74
Tess Bamber (11)	74
Sara Williams (13)	75

William Denham (14)	76
Ashley Williams (13)	76
Ruby Rone (13)	77
Sophie Raymond (13)	77
Callum Griffiths (12)	78
Nicola Tatton (12)	78
Nikita Lewis (13)	79
Hina Bagha (13)	79
Michael Watts (13)	80
Yasmin Nur (13)	80
Becci Rees (13)	81
Adam Sharp (12)	81
Kern Cunningham (11)	82
Kate Lewis (13)	82
Victoria Squire (13)	83
William Squire (11)	83
Tanya Griffiths (13)	84
Barnaby Swift (13)	84
Siân Adams (13)	85
Sophie Dobson (13)	85
Hannah Griffiths (13)	86
Siobhan O'Sullivan (13)	86
Jessica Cale (13)	87
Lisa Owens (12)	87
Catherine Owen (13)	88
Laura Rogers (11)	88
Bethan Rees (13)	89
Jo Davies (12)	89

Tregynon Hall School, Powys

Janette Price (11)	89
Rebecca Williams (15)	90
Avion Warman (15)	90
Dave Mitchell (16)	91
Richard Nichol (14)	91
Matthew Pritchard (14)	92
Callie Skelding (13)	92
Adam Rushton (15)	93
Cori Belliard (16)	93

Whitchurch High School, Cardiff

Katie Davies (11)	94
Aaron Elliott (13)	94
Eve Worrell (11)	95
Steven Freshney (11)	95
Claire Williams (13)	96
Harry Wootten (11)	97
Rebecca Higgins (12)	98
Aimee Yorke (11)	98
Nia Holbrook (13)	99
Hoda Ali Fahiya (11)	99
James Brinning (11)	100
Zayneb Afsar (11)	100
Lee Davis (11)	101
Ellis Jones (11)	101
Juliet Eales (12)	102
Stefanie Rossi (13)	102
Samantha Curtis (13)	103
Megan Sawford (11)	103
Bethan Davies (12)	104
Jemma Evans (12)	104
Emma Standen (11)	105
Lorna Chamberlain (11)	105
Kayleigh Rees (11)	106
Ellis Williams	106
Emily Tuckwell (12)	107
Stacey Harris (12)	107
Sam Lomasney (12)	108
Sam Worrell (13)	108
Ross Wilson (11)	109
Jade Biddlecombe (13)	110
Ben Carey (11)	110
Sophia Gibbs (13)	111
Stephanie Regan (13)	111
Bethan Carr (11)	112
Naomi Morgan (13)	112
Rosemary Jenkins (11)	113
Alys Aston (13)	113
Amy Price (13)	114
Kyle Deek (12)	114
Helen Tucker (14)	115

Sophie Roberts (11)	115
Lauren Roberts (11)	116
Steffan Howells (11)	116
Rachel John (13)	117
Jess Leonard (11)	117
Danny Jones (11)	118
Sophie Standen (12)	118
Tom Skirrow (11)	119
Chloe Davies (11)	119
Menna Davies (11)	120
Sarah Thomas (11)	120
Lia Davies (13)	121
Hannah Joyce (12)	121
Christopher Dench (11)	122
James Tipping (12)	122
Madlen Cartwright (12)	123
Jake Dunn (13)	123
Dan O'Connor (13)	124
Lloyd Davies (12)	124
Rebecca Thomas (12)	124
Emily Irving (11)	125
Liam Creed (11)	125
Owen Lindsey (12)	126
Eleri Cadogan (14)	126
Samantha Bryant (11)	127
Rachel Hanson (13)	128
Charity Muchunga (11)	128
Ellis Morgan (12)	129
Shona Fraser-Skuse (11)	129
Ryan Looker (12)	130
Jac Jones (12)	130
Sam Perkins (11)	131
Hannah Colman (13)	131
Caitlin Davies (13)	132
Danielle Yardley (12)	133
Claire James (12)	133
Josh Carbis (13)	134
David Heslop (11)	134
Jonathan Williams (11)	135
Carys Trace (11)	135
Johanna Lewis (12)	136
Bethan Webber (11)	136

Charlotte Williams (11)	137
Yanni Haralambos (12)	138
Zoe Grima (12)	138
Shakah Meah (11)	138
Megan Hession (11)	139
Thomas Pacey (11)	139
Nader Khundakji (11)	140
Hope Rees (11)	140
Alex Wilson (12)	141
Oliver Jackson (11)	142
Rachel Nealon (12)	142
Charlie Winch (11)	143
Vincent Godfrey (11)	143
Stephanie Ellis (11)	143
Kate Bowley (11)	144
Sarah Jones (11)	144
Jessica Davies (11)	145
Poppy Shillabeer (11)	145
Rebecca Leonard (11)	146
Sarah Gould (11)	146
Dionne Morgans (11)	147
Luke Robson (11)	147
Jordan Sugarman (11)	147
Gareth Lewis (13)	148
Paige Wickers (12)	148
Sophie Baker (11)	149
Elizabeth Shipston (12)	149
Saskia Lehane (11)	150
Catherine Williams (11)	150
Alex Newton (12)	151
Bronwyn Northcott (11)	151
Jamie Kingsford (11)	152
Gabrielle Regan (11)	152
Michael Ley (11)	153
Hannah Lewis (11)	153
Jack Haberfield (11)	154
Jordan Gibbs (11)	154
Alex Amor (11)	155
Vashti Williamson (12)	155
Scott Saunders (12)	156
Ashley Said (11)	156
Bryony James (11)	157

Alun Welsh (12)	157
Bethan Johnston (11)	158
Aimee Harrison (11)	158
Sophie Nash (11)	159
Charlotte Chappell (13)	159
Stevie Morgan (12)	160
Samuel Paul Thomas	160
Kate McCarthy (11)	161
Anna Batten (12)	161
Tom Salmon (11)	162
Rachel Bodger (12)	162
Daniel Draper (12)	163
Timothy Vincent (12)	163
Rhiannon Collins (11)	164
Emma Williams (13)	164
Catherine Stephens (12)	165
Jamie Humphrys (12)	165
Rebeca Evans (12)	166
Kyle Beal (12)	166
Andrew Sleat (13)	167
Scott Curtis (12)	167
William McMahon (12)	168
Tanvir Miah (12)	168
Patrick McDowell (12)	169
Clarice Watkinson (12)	169
Gemma Miles (13)	170
Nick Bond (12)	170
Emma Gill (11)	170
Jack Butler (13)	171
Sophie Davies (13)	171
Ceri Davenport (12)	172
Robyn Pesticcio (13)	172
Harriet Jones (13)	173
Lois Jeremy (13)	174
Holly Venus (14)	174
Phillip Kavanagh (13)	174
Harriet Tangney (13)	175
Charlotte Culliford (12)	175
Rebecca Ann Woodfield (11)	176
Danielle Evans (12)	176
Joshua Yanez (12)	177
Rhiannon Lavin (12)	177

Leigh Jenkins (12)	178
Mark Raicis (12)	179
Kelly Batchelor (12)	179
Lewis Davies (12)	180
Lloyd Davies (12)	180
Ruby Jones (11)	181
Elliott Jones (12)	181
Victoria Grainger (11)	182
Will Morris (12)	182
Harriet Rudden (11)	183
Elizabeth Worby (11)	183
David Harrhy (12)	184
Pauline Parsons (13)	184
Rhiannon Jones (12)	185
Rebecca Shelley (13)	185
Charlotte Marlow (11)	186
Sophie Steele (11)	186
Ellie May Gibbs (12)	187
Jessica Phillips (12)	188
Gareth Bodman (14)	188
Amy Richards (11)	189
Ben Popek (11)	189
Bethan Salaman (14)	190
Christopher Nukes (14)	190
Hanna Brunt (14)	191
Joanna Cawley (14)	191
Fred Rowlands (11)	192
Megan Poley (11)	192
Bryony Acton (11)	193
James Copner (12)	193
Bethan Delve (11)	194
Jessica Puttick (11)	194
Sophie Jones (12)	195
Siân Jones (12)	196
Laura Phelan (12)	196
Frankie Self (13)	197
Adam Jones (14)	197
Ellie Barrow (14)	198
Helena Reid (14)	198
Laura Alice Summerscales (13)	199
Lauren Kelly (14)	199
Craig Perriam (13)	200

Carys Morris (12)	200
Vanessa Hayden (11)	201
Jacob Tucker (14)	202
James Kelly (12)	202
Isabelle Pettersson (12)	203
Tenesiha Allen (13)	203
Claire Nokes (12)	204
Gareth Jones (11)	204
Sara Bodger (12)	205
Harrison Jankovic (12)	205
Rachel Seary (12)	206
Joe Farmer (14)	206
Chris Kavanagh (11)	207
Adam Joslin (11)	207
Caroline Nieuwenhuis (13)	208
Dave Trace (13)	209
Lauren Brobin (12)	209
Tom Coates (13)	210
Michelle Escott (14)	210
Christina Lago (15)	211
Michael Lee (16)	211
Nathan Ashley (14)	212
Alex Foley (13)	212
Rhys James (13)	213
Jermaine Thompson (13)	213
Chris Williams (15)	214
Peter Edward Hughes (11)	214
Charlotte Roberts (13)	215
Chris Harding (14)	215
Gabby James (13)	216
Rebecca Rhind-Jones (12)	216
Henry Gidwell (13)	217
Bo Cordle (13)	217
Emily Chapman (13)	218
Lauren Fisher (11)	218
Sinead Heron (13)	219
Megan Farmer (11)	219
Claire Nieuwenhuis (14)	220
Daniel Thomas (13)	220
Jenny Jenkins (14)	221
Tesni Street (11)	221
Hannah Lago (12)	222

Tom Bishop (14)	222
Nathan Hickery (15)	223
Owen Richards (13)	224
Maddy O'Neill (13)	224
Abbie Ognjenovic (12)	225
Carys Tucker (14)	225
Emma Keenan (12)	226
Emily Knox (11)	226
Charlotte Camilleri (13)	227
Elinor Crawley (12)	227
William Francis (13)	228
Siân Crowley (12)	228
Zoë Azzopardi (12)	229
Jo Pople (13)	229
Emily Harris (13)	230
Alex Kerr (12)	230
Alex McWhirter (13)	230
Kathryn Powell (13)	231
Kate Jenkins (13)	231
Owain Harrison (11)	231
Hannah Jones (12)	232
Erin Stacey (13)	232
Lauren Morgan (12)	233
Saskia Nicolai (12)	233
Tracey Michals (13)	234
Alice Barnes (14)	234
Alexandra Dwyer (12)	235
Sophie Knight (11)	235
Hannah Delaney (12)	236
Lauren Jones (12)	236
David Thomas (11)	236
Rhys McCarthy (11)	237
Daniel Stone (11)	237
Aimee Turner (11)	237
Caroline Boyle (11)	238
Gemma Lloyd (11)	238
Adam Torjussen (11)	239
Jack Shields (11)	239
Bethan Ashford (12)	240
Zakaria Djoudi (11)	240
Hannah Nicholas (12)	241
Leigh Sharman (12)	241

Laura Brewer (12)	242
Aneurin Campbell (11)	242
Amy Deering (11)	242
Bryn William Rogers (11)	243
Alun Cadogan (11)	243
Liam Venus (11)	243
Jessica Hall (14)	244
Lily Cleall-Harding (11)	244
Diva Deane (11)	245
Alexandra Bond (11)	245
Krystal Mills (11)	246
Jessica Bishop (11)	246
Gemma Fitzgibbon (13)	246
Samantha Boothroyd (14)	247
Joanne Bloom (11)	247
Kelly Shaw (11)	248
Cameron Stacey (11)	248

Ysgol Gyfun Bro Myrddin, Carmarthenshire
Kayley Davies-Richards (17)	249
Hannah Jones (17)	250

The Poems

Nestlé - Making A Killing

How could you force upon the lives of the poor,
A debt that killed babies in the midst of war?
You gave out free milk to stop mothers producing,
The babies needed more while your profits were boosting.
The young were dying, but you were still earning,
Hearts were bleeding but you were yearning,
For money, this greed, it sickens us now,
All we can ask is why? And how?

The laws that you break are there for a reason,
But they don't apply when it's *you* up for treason,
Murdering children would cost me my life,
Murdering children just sharpens your knife.
And gives you the edge, the one that you need,
To conquer the masses of western greed,
With your products that give you a third of the wealth,
That others work hard for in these lands of ill-health.

How many laws have you managed to crawl around?
You've taken lives but profits have turned around,
All of this hardship and all of this grief,
So you can steal money like a common thief,
It's hard to hear who backs and who hates you,
Countries have declared it but no one will stop you,
So what will it take to end this injustice?
What will it take to curb this malpractice?

From the poor in the dirt who needed your help,
You charged them for more and took for yourself,
Countless times you practised this crime,
Who fought for them then? We'll fight this time.

Joe Coleman (15)
Brecon High School, Powys

If . . .

If my brother were an animal he would be a mighty lion
His teeth would glow like the sun
His chin as rough as sandpaper, his claws razor-sharp
His mane bends in the direction of the wind
His rough gold coat glows in the sunlight.

He bounds after his prey snaking through the thick, tall grasses
His steps shaking the ground, his lips dripping with water
which splashes on the ground.

His roar echoes off the snow-covered mountains
His bulging eyes lighting up the darkness as he stalks
                                    his evening meal
He laps up the water into his mouth and swallows it with grace.

As he walks through the jungle his powerful legs snap
the fallen branches in half.
Rodents and birds hurry away, scared that they might be
his next victim.
This is my brother, the mighty lion!

Rhys Burgess (12)
Brecon High School, Powys

Storm

Silently he sleeps way up high,
But when he gets angry he makes destruction up in the sky.
Thunder is a vicious wolf with long, sharp claws,
Up in the sky it howls and roars.
Lightning, an evil man electricity charged,
When his bolts of lightning strike the ground
They make the most terrific sound.
A beautiful woman with tears of rain,
Will the sun ever shine again?
The tornado with terrifying breath twisting round and round,
Nothing can safely stay on the ground.
When the storm starts to calm down,
The sun comes out like a golden crown.

Dafydd Maclennan (11)
Brecon High School, Powys

The Weather

The weather can be bad
Very bad, he's almost mad
But he can be very good
He can't be brilliant, maybe he could

This poem is about the weather
Some of his friends all together
This poem isn't the best
But it is better than the rest.

The sun she hovers very high
Very high above the sky
She glares down at the earth
And fills hearts with joy and mirth

The wind blows round and round
He blows very hard and gives the earth a pound
He flies for miles and miles
He takes the earth from her smiles.

David Jenkins (12)
Brecon High School, Powys

Fire

In her red and golden cloak,
With blazing orange hair,
Dancing in the fireplace,
And leaping up the wood,
Throwing balls of fire,
At anything she can reach.
Her long tongue reaching out,
Licking at the walls,
A crackling voice shouting,
To stay away from her.
Feed her coal and wood,
And she'll warm you once again,
But throw over some water,
And she'll hiss and hide away.

Molly Owen (11)
Brecon High School, Powys

Freedom

I feel pity for the blades of grass
All rooted to the ground,
How they must long for freedom,
Albeit never found.

Oh, how I'd love to be a bird
And soar into the sky,
Or to be the vibrant flames
Who dance until they die.

I wish that I could fly away
And live up in the clouds,
And float around all night and day
And never come back down.

But then my dreams all fall away
And I am forced to see
The truth of it, harsh and cold,
My own reality.

For I am like those blades of grass,
I'm always tied down,
And the freedom that I'm looking for
Will never come around.

Zoë Crane (15)
Brecon High School, Powys

If . . .

If my friend were like water
What form would she take?
As a stream that is gentle
Or an icy blue lake.

As a raindrop that stings
On your face when it rains
Or as one that just trickles
Down glass windowpanes.

As a river that bends
With a turn and a twist
Washing softly the pebbles
In the cold morning mist.

As a calm pond in summer
Glistening warm in the sun
As a deep raging sea
When winter's begun.

A reflection in these
Of my friend I can see
And I wonder, I wonder
How does she see me?

Ffion Miles (12)
Brecon High School, Powys

Stars

Small and silver
Shiny and bright
How beautiful they
Shine in the night.

In their silver gowns
They dance in the night
They glare at things
And make them shine bright.

Dancing, dancing
Round and round
The moon is their
Big disco ball.

O, they're not out tonight
Well I'm not surprised
Partying five nights
In a row.

Elin Rees (11)
Brecon High School, Powys

The Stars

The shining stars in the sky,
Gaze down from up high,
With their silvery faces and their shining cloaks,
Eyes that glow with joy and hope.
Each night they shine down on Earth,
To give the people light and worth.
Some nights the dark, gloomy clouds appear,
Which gives the people a sense of fear.
They dance and glitter through the night,
Bobbing around like a kite,
Shooting stars shimmer like fish,
If you see one, make a wish,
Just for us they're scattered about,
We hope they never go out.

Alwyn Lee (11)
Brecon High School, Powys

Fire

He dances and crackles, and leaps athletically,
In his trail of rage is a place you wouldn't want to be.
A man covered in flames, a cloak of red and gold,
He will help you a lot, if you're surrounded by cold.
If you can tame him, he will be your friend,
But if you can't control him, destruction he might send.
He is allied with dark smoke, and also blistering heat,
Now here is a threesome, you wouldn't like to meet.
Smoke is a woman, grey hair and clothes,
She can choke you to death, but fresh air she loathes.
Heat is another woman, who loves the fire and sun,
She wears yellow and orange, you'll never have won.
In his spreading rage he sometimes brings despair,
With fiery tongues of flame, licking at the air.

Alun Davies (12)
Brecon High School, Powys

The Sun

The sun is massive,
He is red-hot,
He has the colour of yellow and orange,
And he gives people nice tans,
And he grows everything in the spring and summer.
All of the lambs and the flowers and everything,
He's bright and makes me smile,
And I wish he was there every day of the year,
Instead of the snow, rain, wind and thunder.
Every time he goes down the moon comes up,
And when the moon goes down the sun comes up.
In the end he does have to leave us,
And the winter comes instead and takes over Sun's place.

Rhys Nicholls (11)
Brecon High School, Powys

Winter

Deep beneath the mountainside
The mighty dragon begins to rise.
Slowly he lifts his majestic head
Crawling from his leafy bed.
For now is his time to strive once more
Blizzards forming in his paw.
Then this power he shall send
To create the autumn's end.

Now he shall rule the winds again
The drifts, the hail and the rain.
Though the autumn may resist
It bears no match for his frozen fist.
And as he bellows his almighty roar
A deep grey storm cloud he shall draw.
No plant shall stand to Winter's wrath
Few leaves standing in his path.

As he leaps up in the air
Autumn returns to his lair.
Winter swooping in the sky
Chilling creatures passing by.
For now the autumn is destroyed
The winter snow can be enjoyed.

From under his wings
Snowflakes sing . . .
Twirling
Swirling
Whirling
Curling

As the frozen beast draws on
Crystals forming from his yawn.
Cutting through the clear still night
The sparkling stars glistening bright.
Over islands he does fly
Lighting up the pitch-black sky.
With the Northern Lights
A glint from his eye . . .

Purples
Greens
Blues
And golds . . .
Forming from a beast so cold.

Frostbite he does send to gnaw
Produce from his mighty claw.
He sends hail in endless sleets
Freezing rain; icy sheets.
High reaching mountains looking bleak
And the havoc fast floods can wreak
Are often forgotten by those near the hearth
Who can escape Winter's wrath . . .

But when old Winter is tired and worn
The dragon of spring may begin his new dawn
For a simple young shoot pushing through
May mean little to me or you
But for poor old Winter 'tis time to retreat to his lair
Where until next Winter he will lie undisturbed there . . .

Poetic and magical this season can be
For that is what Winter means to me.

Emily Ham (13)
Brecon High School, Powys

Thunder And Lightning

Two brothers in the sky
Creating storms, here's why;
One is a whiner having a tantrum,
The other scolds him, he acts like his mum.
Thunder is thumping the clouds, but it is feeble,
For Lightning stitches the damage with a zigzag needle.
And that is how they make a storm,
It's a pity they were even born.

Dafydd Reeves (12)
Brecon High School, Powys

Fireworks

Suddenly the night sky is alight,
Filled with a fiery scene,
Gleaming and glowing, sparkling lights,
Everyone's childhood dream.

Rockets and Roman candles,
Catherine wheels as well,
Breathtaking colours,
With a story to tell.

The horizon is bursting,
Wherever you turn,
Rubies and sapphires,
All waiting to burn.

The whole night is magical,
A miracle unfolds,
Though brief in their beauty,
The fireworks thrill us all.

Such transient beauty,
Dressing the autumn sky,
Laughter and screaming,
Reaching a note so high.

An event to remember,
Darkness fills with light,
Oh, how we truly cherish,
Our bonfire night.

Hassan Izzat (13)
St Michael's School, Dyfed

Great Minds

'Great mind!' they said to me,
'You can count to infinity!'
I blushed bright crimson,
But hastened to add,
'To infinity and beyond!'

'Great mind!' they said to me,
'You can spell any word.
So come on, let's see,
Spell any word that has more than 10 letters.'
So, for a few seconds, I faltered and then, stammering, said,
'D-e-o-x-y-r-i-b-o-n-u-c-l-e-i-c-a-c-i-d.'

'Great mind!' they said to me,
'What about your languages?'
And so I whispered,
'Lo que lingua gefällt vous.'
They looked at me in amazement,
And so I translated,
'Whatever language pleases you,
'Spanish, Italian, German, French?'

And so they pestered,
Do this, do that,
The words, 'great mind'
Ringing in my ears.

But they are only voices,
Voices I cannot believe,
Voices in my head.

Harriet Clark (13)
St Michael's School, Dyfed

My Mum

My mum is amazing
She does everything
She cooks, cleans and shops
And still has time to love me.

My mum is the best
She watches me play my sport
When I get injured
She nurses me back to full health.

My mum is super
When I do my homework
And when I get stuck
She is there to lend a hand.

I can't say much more about my mum
Apart from she's the best
In the whole wide world.

Tom Townsend (13)
St Michael's School, Dyfed

My Dog

I have a lovely pet -
It is a little dog,
I took him to the vet
When he ate a frog.

We couldn't stop him hopping;
He really was a sight;
His tummy started dropping
It gave us such a fright!

When the vet did see him
He gave the dog a squeeze,
There is no frog inside him
He must be covered in fleas!

Stephanie Turner (13)
St Michael's School, Dyfed

Monsieur Hugo

Monsieur Hugo he is called
But he isn't a Frenchman
Nor a man at all.
He is my dog
A dog he'll always be;
Not a wicked warthog
That reeks of decay,
Not a crow that glides with ease
My dog is none of they.
He is a dog who
Loves to play with
His bone, alone. It is true
That my dog does not
Think he is a dog.
He does not like other dogs a lot
But prefers human friends
To wag his tail when he
Sees them coming round the bend
Of the drive that leads to my home.
Back to his name, Monsieur Hugo
Was so called when Glyn phoned
And asked about the dog we found
At the dog's home.
'Hugo's a funny name for a hound,'
He said. I replied,
'It's French. We chose it because
It sounds quite posh,' I lied.
'Well if he's French I'll call
Him Monsieur Hugo,'
He stalled,
And put the phone down.
I stroked his coat so warm, so soft.
Hugo *is* a funny name for a hound.

Greg Powles (13)
St Michael's School, Dyfed

Fireworks

Fireworks of red, blue and emerald-green
Flashes of yellow, gold and ultramarine
The most technicolour you've ever seen
Zooming and soaring in the sky, looking obscene.

They whiz flamboyantly in the air
They whip, they flip and ripple your hair.

Fireworks so bright and beautiful igniting the night sky
They lift your spirits making you want to fly
On the ground they sizzle and stir, ready to release
They shake and shudder, like a dog on a leash.

So bright and glorious fireworks might be
But be careful or you might pay a pricey fee
Fireworks can burn, scold and even kill
Take their risks at your will.

Kueni Victor Igbagiri (13)
St Michael's School, Dyfed

Saturday Morning

It is light outside and I know it's Saturday morning
Because on weekdays it is dark, damp, dismal and early.
I jump up and have a shower,
I will be at my piano lesson in half an hour.

Saturday morning is a time to catch up
On sleep, phone calls, emails and meeting with friends.
Go to town looking at clothes I wish I had,
Then it's time for tennis and I am picked up by my dad.

This is what happens nearly every Saturday morning,
A great big rush to get things done.
Even though Saturday morning is not much of a rest,
It is definitely the best.

Ruth Fletcher (13)
St Michael's School, Dyfed

Angry Fireworks

A burning ball of angry fire,
Was ignited inside a stubborn mind,
Its fierce flames and nasty flickers
Were boldly building and quickly binding.

A tiny dot shot extremely high,
His face turned deepest red,
The wind was fierce in the sky,
Gritted teeth, clenched fists, his anger nearly bled.

Crash, bang, dazzling bright,
A booming wail and yell was let out,
The sparkling colour, crackled light,
The exploding frustration fled straight out.

The wind that howled, jaded,
After the deafening shout and roar,
The fireworks that did rip through the sky, faded,
And a quivering body stood drained, with no strength or courage
                                                      left to bawl.

Lucy Jeffery (13)
St Michael's School, Dyfed

Fireworks

Fireworks shoot up into the dark sky,
They then explode releasing their magical wonders,
We gaze at their wonderful flashes of light,
Then the dark sky swallows up the bright flashes.

Soon swirl around without a care,
Others make noises which echo in the sky,
The rest release a fountain of sparks which embraces itself,
But their last minute of life is a great one.

It releases its powers and then dies,
The ashes gently land onto the soft ground,
There it stays forgotten while the wind blows,
Watching its own kind release their wonders and die.

Faaz Ashraf (13)
St Michael's School, Dyfed

Great Minds - Churchill

Churchill was a bold man,
A strong man,
A wise man,
He did not waver from his plan.

He warned of Hitler, of Nazis,
Who listened?
Nobody at all,
They called him a fool, a liar.

Then came the day when at last
It came true,
Was it too late?
Had he been ignored for too long?

He spoke of Britain's finest hour,
He lifted the nation,
He kept them alive,
A great mind in every respect.

But what could we learn from
Such a great mind?
I will tell you,
Never give in, never, never, never!

Lloyd Hopkin (13)
St Michael's School, Dyfed

Great Minds - Haiku

Working all the time,
Composing and inventing.
Look at what they've done.

Amina Hussain (13)
St Michael's School, Dyfed

My Pet Humans

My name is Mia,
A pedigree cat,
Daughter of two champions,
That won fifty contests,
Or something like that.

My first pet's a human,
Miss Neat-Holmes is her name,
I love to scratch her sofa,
She sold me,
Don't know why.

Mr Pot is my next pet,
I love to rip up that flowerbed,
Which he makes just for me,
But he went mad and put me up for sale,
What did I do wrong?

I went to Mrs Maternal next,
I loved to play with her eight babies,
We played scratching, scramming, biting games,
She gave me away,
Why?

Now I'm in a boring dogs' home,
No one wants to buy me,
I'm a pedigree cat you know,
Come and buy me,
I promise I'll be good.

Josephine Dingley (13)
St Michael's School, Dyfed

My Dog Milkshake

He came to us three days ago,
A glossy, golden ball.
With eyes that shone and glimmered
And only two weeks old.

He played in sun, he played in rain,
He was quite a nutter.
Chewed toys scattered on the rug,
And paw prints in the butter.

Neighbours, salesmen, postmen, milkmen
Try and avoid his bite.
Naughty, vicious, always bad,
Why couldn't he be polite?

He got his name in McDonald's -
There was a small earthquake,
My drink spilt all over him,
So now he's called Milkshake!

Parvathy Vipulendran (13)
St Michael's School, Dyfed

My Mum

My mum, a gentle, loving person,
Always saying, 'Have you got this?
Have you got that?' - always fussing.

My mum, she never sits down,
She's always on the go, doing this,
Doing that, she never stops.

My mum is a happy person, never down,
She could smile for Britain,
Except when she shouts at me.

My mum, to sum her up, let's say
She's kind all over,
Never says a nasty thing.

Ashley Eynon-Davies (13)
St Michael's School, Dyfed

Fireworks

Soaring high, a dart of fire.
Crack! The skies erupt.
Glowing rain - weightless,
Disappears in an instant.

Splutter, spitter,
A fumarole ignites:
A sea of colour and glitter,
Cascading in their flight.

Fountains: glowing, sparkling,
Crackle and frizzle. Bursting
Like corked champagne.

Wheels alight spin and scream,
Varying colours: crimson to green.
Beautiful. Till life burns out.
In death its colour is black as night.

Sally Scourfield (13)
St Michael's School, Dyfed

Saturday Morning

I like Saturday mornings
When I don't have to get out of bed,
Rush to the bathroom
And wake my sleepy head.

I like Saturday mornings
When I can get up and watch TV,
Like 'Tom and Jerry' acting crazy,
When I'm eating lots of sweets and being lazy.

I like Saturday mornings
When I don't have to put my school uniform on,
Wear what I want and go out and have some
Fun! Fun! Fun!

Kristian Hickin (13)
St Michael's School, Dyfed

Great Minds In The Making

Thomas Edison's inventions were big and small,
The most famous was the light bulb giving electricity to all.
Two others worth a mention changed our leisure time around,
Motion pictures gave us movies and the gramophone its sound.

Alexander Fleming also made a great contribution,
As a microbiologist he offered a solution.
To the many illnesses during that era,
He discovered that penicillin could destroy bacteria.

Albert Einstein, a man of great renown,
His theory of relativity amazed all who were around.
He was against nuclear destruction and its affect on mankind,
Acutely aware that it was discovered by his own brilliant mind.

These great minds now are all gone,
I wonder how many more are to come.
If we all work hard, you never know,
Our young minds will change and hopefully grow.
One day we might be great,
One day we might not make it.
But let's get back to learning now,
We have our chance - let's take it.

Rachel Llewellyn (13)
St Michael's School, Dyfed

Fireworks

My mum is like a firework,
All ready and waiting until it's time to explode.
When she gets going,
No one will ever stop her,
Unless somebody gets in her way,
And she'll go off with a crackle and a hiss.
She'll keep going until she burns out,
And when she ends,
The person in the way had better watch out,
Bang!

Barnaby Rees-Jones (13)
St Michael's School, Dyfed

Fireworks On November The 5th

I walked out into the garden, excited as ever before
                                       on November the 5th.
My eyes were drawn to the moonlit sky
Upon which the trees were beautifully silhouetted

Whoosh
Wham
Bang
They were off!
The sky and garden alike were lit up by all of the colours
                                       of the spectrum,
Reds, blues, greens and purples
There were all sorts of shapes and sizes.

Whoosh
Wham
Bang
Then came the next lot
Even more spectacular than the last
It seemed as though the sparkling and shining would continue forever.

Whoosh
Wham
Bang

Then it was over
Just as quickly as it started it was over
We stood and gazed into the warming bonfire
It was then I began to think, it will be another year, another orbit
                                       around the sun before we can witness
Fireworks on November the 5th again.

Matthew Watkins (13)
St Michael's School, Dyfed

The North Pole

The biting blizzard cuts through snow,
Hear the perishing wind blow.
It dances passionately on lakes,
A moaning, whistling sound it makes.

The shimmering aurora shines bright,
It fills and revives the silent night.
The ravishing stars fill the sky,
Almost touchable but still too high.

The wilderness of snow covers land,
The honourable mountains are grand.
The blistering cold makes you shiver,
The bleak winds makes you quiver.

The snowflakes are small and faint,
This place is a masterpiece, filled with paint.
Crunchy snow, feel the air that is cold,
The mysterious wonders of the North Pole.

Tanu Verma (13)
St Michael's School, Dyfed

Fireworks

Colours flying through the sky,
Beauty money cannot buy,
All colliding in the air,
Everyone cannot help but stare and stare.

The noise is like a massive smash
Or like a loud, huge crash,
It makes all pets shiver with fear,
But all we do is cheer.

The colours finally fell to earth,
We thought we'd got our money's worth,
As everybody leaves us alone,
The image will be with us until we are grown.

James Prosser (13)
St Michael's School, Dyfed

Winter Fun

The howling wind in the winter,
Straightens the spines of blades of grass.
Cold as the icicles strung on window sills,
It stings the trees and plants.

When everyone sleeps at night,
It covers the ground which once was dry.
The brown trees are painted white,
Mountains and hills are covered in powdery white.

Children play in the snow,
Make snowmen and snowball fights.
Everyone has fun and joy,
The air is full of Christmas lights.

The winter fun and joy will end,
Though spring smiles will begin.
The winter will give way to spring,
With hope the birds will sing.

Shruti Uppala (13)
St Michael's School, Dyfed

My Mum

My mum has a great mind,
Hair as black as the night,
A voice as gentle as can be,
A loving, caring person are all her qualities.

A mind as sharp as a razor,
As quick as an eagle in flight,
A popular medical graduate,
Her heart is as pure as white.

Her presentations draw attention,
An expert it is often said,
How proud I am of my mum:
My mother, my guide, my friend.

Waleed Khalik (14)
St Michael's School, Dyfed

Primary School

Ah! The good old days in primary school!
Not much work,
Lots of fun,
Especially licking lush lollies in the summer sun.

Ah! The good old days in primary school!
Playing in the park,
Picking leaves off trees as we pass,
And lolling about on the freshly mown grass.

Ah! The good old days in primary school!
Exploring through nature's world,
Feeling the smoothness of the bird's feather,
Listening to a cricket bat hitting leather.

Ah! The good old days in primary school!
But sadly we all grew up,
We knew around the corner secondary school lurks,
Way more work, but considerably less perks.

Now when I come home from school, my sisters ask,
'Please can you come to play?'
But I have to reply;
'Sorry I have too much work to do today!'

Viraj Ratnalikar (13)
St Michael's School, Dyfed

Saturday Morning

Saturday morning is the cold side of my pillow
Saturday is breakfast in bed
Saturday is no school
Saturday is sorting out the shed.

Saturday is watching a film
Saturday is meeting your friends
Saturday is having fun
Saturday is a day that never ends.

Falling into ice wild water
Dripping down a cold neckline
Sliding through a water slide tunnel
Saturday surfboard shrine.

Pedalling a fat horse uphill
Downhill cheetah pulling me by its tail
Cycling across the earthquake bridle path
Saturday freedom not for sale.

Saturday night is watching old Parky
Saturday night is getting ready for homework
Saturday night is stretching on a massaging sofa
Where thoughts of next Saturday lurk and smirk.

Kristian Limpert (13)
St Michael's School, Dyfed

Change

Feelings change, people change,
Everything changes,
Everything except you.
You're the same now
As you were back then,
So long ago,
You'll never change.

I keep hoping that
Someday, somehow
There'll be a glimmer of hope,
In the darkest corners of your mind,
That your heart will melt
From its stone prison,
And become able to love,
But that's impossible for you;
You'll never change.

Maybe one day, years from today,
You'll feel the same way.
You'll want someone to change for you,
To feel the love you'll never know.
I'm still waiting, you know that, and yet
You just stand there, lost in your mind.
This wait won't end now, not ever,
You'll never change.

Ryan Bowen (14)
St Michael's School, Dyfed

Saturday Morning

The wolves are howling
to the now gone moon:
the gloomy forest dressed like an old lady
ready to go to sleep
in her long brown robe.

Christmas carols
carried by the wind
from a lonely cottage:
in the snowy mountains
like gigantic Christmas puddings
covered with sweet glazing.

The birds singing
their merry songs;
in the flowery trees
like multicoloured hands
trying to reach for the blue sky.

The cows mooing
to each other;
in the infinite fields
touched by the silent wind
like waves out of a green sea.

Andrea Bertelli (13)
St Michael's School, Dyfed

Your Mum

She loves you when you're weak,
Supports you when you're strong,
Applauds you when you're right,
Helps you when you're wrong.

Even when you argue,
Even when you light,
She loves you always,
Thinks of you every night.

Taken for granted when she's there,
But you realise when she's gone,
That sometimes you should
Stick the kettle on.

Don't tell your friends,
Because you maybe shy,
That you love your mum,
Until the end of time.

Not always eye to eye,
Sometimes she'll make you cry,
But that doesn't mean a thing,
Because you are her life, her all, her everything.

Atif Sabah (13)
St Michael's School, Dyfed

Fireworks

Whoosh!

Up it shot,
To the huge, vast blackness of the night sky,
The unexplored beyond.

Brushing aside the resistance of the winds
As it soared, soared, soared.

Bang!

As it curled
Into a magnificent, fiery flower
Brighter than the sun.

Powering past the ever-growing darkness
As it shone, shone, shone.

Ah!

The crowd sighed
Crackling, roaring, echoing through the night
Drawing the applause.

It gave the night sky a peaceful, soothing glow
As it died, died, died.

Christopher Pavlou (13)
St Michael's School, Dyfed

The Seasons

Autumn
Falling leaves in shades of brown
Swept by the wind, go swirling around
Birds fly south and the nights close in
Winter will very shortly begin.

Winter
Icy mornings, Jack Frost is about
It's time I got my warm coat out
The storms will come and the snow will fall
This is the season that is the least fun of all.

Spring
April showers will come and go
The warmer winds will now begin to blow
Flowers and trees will burst into life
My favourite season is now in sight.

Summer
The days are long and the skies are blue
And the owl calls out tu-whit tu-whoo
The sun shines down and warms my skin
Very soon school holidays will begin.

Sophie Adams (13)
St Michael's School, Dyfed

My Budgies

My green one arrived one autumn day
tagged and lonely I heard Mum say . . .
perching high upon the arm I made
in the shiny house that had been laid.

Day after day no sound is heard
a worrying time for all concerned
'What do we do?' I hear the cry
another one we must buy.

Off we go down tarmaced road
a wonderful sight we will behold
white one, white one, they all decide;
let's hope this is the final ride.

Home we get, time to see
if we have done the right deed -
days passed, one by one, then suddenly
it has begun . . .

A glorious sound, pitch on pitch
our investment has done the trick
two happy souls, now tweet away
content, and happy day by day.

Rhiân Hughes (14)
St Michael's School, Dyfed

My Pet

It gazed pitifully from within the shabby cardboard box,
Eyes dull as unlit charcoal,
Matted hair and bitten ear shadowing the light.
Fear clouded the beauty of its eyes,
Yet something compelling flickered from within,
More powerful than all else.

The judge stood intently with a scrutinising gaze,
Each dog majestic and proud.
One champion shone resplendent,
Eyes burning like fired glass,
Coat gleaming as the finest silk.
To this he gave the prize.

From matted hair to gleaming coat,
Her beauty reigned supreme,
The spirit never wavered once,
In my beloved dog.

Bethany Sawyer (13)
St Michael's School, Dyfed

Fireworks

Spinning, whizzing, sizzling
Flying through the air
Like an acrobat, making his final jump
Delicately, but fast. Gliding through the air
Flashing and banging
Sparks fly from lit fireworks
Some dance in the air
Some fizz on the ground
A display of fireworks
With magical colours
Hitting the crisp, dark sky
Mixing with the silver stars.

Jessica Davies (13)
St Michael's School, Dyfed

My Cat

In the winter she is so lazy,
She eats so much and stays in all day,
Now she is a fat cat.

In the summer her hunting skills are so handy,
She eats in the morning and goes out all day,
Now she is as thin as a rake.

Her bright green eyes so useful,
Her ears can hear the slightest of sounds,
Her soft paws as quiet as a mouse,
Her slender, sleek, streamlined body, so fast,
Then she crouches ready to pounce,
Got it, she plays with the mouse and eats it.

She comes home at night, so pleased with herself,
Sitting proud, her coat gleaming.

Lisa Tucker (13)
St Michael's School, Dyfed

15th Century Genius

Sitting alone in his study as the clock strikes twelve,
Scribbling notes in the candlelight.
They call his science 'blasphemy'
But he has to know, he can't let this go.
This world keeps going forever -
He wants to know why we cannot as well,
Always seeking answers to his illegal questions,
Knowing that one day his so-called madness may be rewarded.
He will live - and die - for that day.
He realises that everything that lives may serve a purpose -
He determines to make this his.

The candle flickers and dies,
He lays down his pen.
But in the dark his mind sparks on.

Nikita Poli (13)
St Michael's School, Dyfed

My Mum

My mum nags and nags,
Tidy your room,
Do your homework,
Wash your face,
Eat up your veggies,
She just nags and nags.

Every day, every hour,
Every minute, every second,
At this, at that,
At everything,
She just nags and nags.

My mum nags at me,
She nags at dad,
She nags at the dog,
She nags at everyone,
She just nags and nags.

She can laugh,
She can smile,
She can cry,
She can sing,
But she just can't stop nagging.

Jenny Sze (13)
St Michael's School, Dyfed

The Wind

Howling, howling, the cry of the wind
Driving down the road
Then crashes into trees
It flies in the air like a dart hitting a dartboard
The wind frightened the kids sleeping in their beds
It leaps over hurdles like an athlete in the Olympics
It slams like a basketball going in a hoop.

Owain Bladen (12)
Sir Thomas Picton School, Haverfordwest

The Wind

An enchantress song she sings
Flying on invisible wings
On the treetops all around
Touching Heaven and the ground
Dancing through the garden plants
Whispering silently to the ants

She changes her song and it picks up pace
She races all around the place
She punches trees
And shakes the leaves
She uproots plants
And throws the ants

Then once again she floats around
The tranquil spirit on the ground
Dancing on hills and over streams
An enchantress song she sings
Over oceans, above the mountains
Singing and dancing through the fountains.

Connor George (12)
Sir Thomas Picton School, Haverfordwest

The Wind

It's as strong as an ox
Tough as old boots.

Beats up houses taking slates off the roof
With an almighty hoof.

As quick as a whippet after a rabbit
It sounds like a dog barking at a parrot.

It looks like the world's strongest boy.

Sam Parry (12)
Sir Thomas Picton School, Haverfordwest

The Demons

The rain ran swiftly down the side of the old house,
The rotten wood that barricaded the windows was hanging off
And the rain dribbled down it,
The dark twisted ivy topped the house and the rain drained down it,
The shadows that lay around the house were as black as coal
As if someone had put a dark spell around them,
Or some demon was at work in them.

The traveller stood there pleased to have found shelter,
The rain trickled down his weathered cloak and his hood was dripping,
He slowly walked up to the house,
As he reached the black door, he gave one loud thump against it,
Silence continued,
Until he threw his body at the doors, they flew open,
He stepped inside.

The house was in dead silence,
Only the sound of the beating bothered breath of some
Other thing in the room,
The demons blood-red eyes watched him as if trying to chase
Him out of the house,
They spoke in his mind as if trying piercing hope instead of skin,
Soon the traveller fled leaving the demons to sleep.

George Davies (13)
Sir Thomas Picton School, Haverfordwest

Feelings

I feel scornful, secluded and sadness,
Miserable, mournful and meaningless,
I feel lonely, lost and low,
The pain, the hate the woe,
I feel dejected, downcast and desolate,
The rage not gone away yet,
I feel so isolated, inane and ill,
The wind and its icy chill,
You feel . . .
You feel nothing.

Josh Balfe (14)
Sir Thomas Picton School, Haverfordwest

Shall I Or Shan't I?

'Come inside,'
An echoed voice,
Shall I or shan't I?
It's a difficult choice!

The floorboards creaked,
A sudden squeak,
Was I wrong to step inside?
Should I run? Should I hide?

A cool breeze passed,
The breath I took, would be my last?
Will I ever get out?
Shall I cry? Shall I shout?

'Come inside'
An echoed voice,
Shall I or shan't I?
I'd made the choice!

Laurie Williams (13)
Sir Thomas Picton School, Haverfordwest

The Wind

The wind is travelling around the town,
Blowing through the trees,
Leaping, rushing everywhere,
Picking up the rustling leaves,
It does not seem to have a care,
Never still, never dead,
Whirling past my spinning head,
Always moving, always alive,
Howling, whistling as it walks on by,
The wind, a stranger in the town,
Wearing its cold winter gown,
Trying to rest for a little while,
And then nowhere to be heard or seen,
Finally, calmly settles to sleep.

Charlotte Butcher (12)
Sir Thomas Picton School, Haverfordwest

The Wind

The wind is hustling through the night,
Giving everyone a fright,
Jumping, leaping through the air,
Stripping every tree quite bare.

The wind is twirling through the town,
Making a tremendous sound,
Piercing, whistling night and day,
It blows all others out of the way.

The wind smacks every windowpane,
It hits it just like the rain,
It dances around on its toes,
Pushing bushes with its blows.

The wind is hustling through the night,
Giving everyone a fright,
Jumping, leaping through the air,
Stripping every tree quite bare.

Natalie Richards (13)
Sir Thomas Picton School, Haverfordwest

The Wind

Angrily she rattles at doors
Trying to get in
She does not succeed and in her anger overturns the bin
She swims over houses and trees
Pulling off the leaves
As they gently fall to the ground
They are picked up by invisible fingers and sent swirling all around.

She dances through streets
Sweeping up dead leaves and litter
But in her mind the thoughts are bitter.

The next morning all is gone
There is no trace of what has been going on.

Katy Evans (12)
Sir Thomas Picton School, Haverfordwest

The Wind

The wind blows a cold quivering air,
That howls and moves everywhere.
Mouth widens and sadly whistles,
As it runs passed and brushes the thistles.

A sudden breeze to a roaring gust,
Tired but determined to carry on, I must.
Sweeping the leaves, creaking the doors,
Hands are sweaty, feet have got sores.

The wind grows strong, it is setting a pace,
Gathering speed to win a race.
Its pulse beats fast, it is getting stronger,
Destroying things as it carries on longer.

I stretch ahead, I can see the line,
Now the wind gets calm, satisfied with its time.
Arms spread out panting for breath,
It seems like the wind's coming to its death.

Autumn, winter, spring and summer,
The wind has power, like a long distance runner.

Christina Morgan (12)
Sir Thomas Picton School, Haverfordwest

The Wind

The wind has a punch,
That will blow away your lunch,
As it dances around the beach,
You can hear a cold screech,
It squirms through the cracks in the door,
Like a cold, icy war,
It crashes the pictures which are blown off the walls,
You can hear the rolling of the footballs,
So this is what happens in the night,
So be careful where you fly your kite.

Poppy Purcell (12)
Sir Thomas Picton School, Haverfordwest

What Will Happen Next?

The bombs lit the streets as light as day,
There was rubble all around,
People running like herds of wild bulls,
The plane flew overhead,
It dropped high from the sky, directly onto our house.

I felt scared, worried,
I could feel and taste,
The dirty dust in my mouth,
My mother was distraught,
And my dad was running low on comfort.

I was thinking,
I was lucky,
My family and I,
Were all fine,
And so were my pets.

The different swish of the wind,
Told me that nothing would ever be the same,
The weightlessness of the dust,
Floating in and out of my mouth,
What will happen next?

Laura Williams (12)
Sir Thomas Picton School, Haverfordwest

The Wind

The wind runs across the land
Spiralling like a spring
You can't catch him
He will catch you
You can't eat him
He will eat you
You can't beat him
He will beat you
He dances around and
Around and around.

Luke Buntwal (13)
Sir Thomas Picton School, Haverfordwest

Someone's In The Shadows

The wind howled like a young wolf lost in a lonely forest,
Light from the full moon shone brightly through the curtains.

Someone's in the shadow.

I can hear faint footsteps,
They come towards me.

Someone's in the shadow.

I turn when I hear the creak,
I look, waiting for a great grey ghost to enter.

Someone's in the shadow.

But nothing, there was nothing,
Except for the faint sound of a dripping tap.

Someone's in the shadow.

I walk in the direction of the bathroom,
I push open the heavy, wooden door.

Someone's in the shadow.

A loud bang echoed through the house,
It startled me,
I run.

Someone's in the shadow.

I run down the stairs,
The front door was open,
Now I know.

Someone's in the house.

Rachel Davies (13)
Sir Thomas Picton School, Haverfordwest

The Haunted House

The wandering stranger walks out at ten o'clock
And ends up at number 13 London Road,
Here stands a battered middle-aged house on the edge of town
That no one has dared to go inside
Until now.

He slips in through the torn down doors,
And firstly goes to the dark living room
Where he sees a portrait of the last owner
That was dated 1827,
Next, to the kitchen where he sees a stove,
That was used many years ago.

He said, 'This house isn't haunted at all, I think I'll stay,'
But a heartbeat later, he saw a bright light.

He screamed and left his things there,
Ran as fast as he could out of the courtyard,
Flew out of the gate,
And never went there again.

Bryan Power (13)
Sir Thomas Picton School, Haverfordwest

The Wind

As the wind slowly fights its way
through the alleys and streets.
People close their doors to his face
as he leaps over gates and fence
and taps at windows and doors.
He startles people on bikes
by coming up behind them and shouting *boo!*
He dances up the chimney
and crashes through the letterbox.
He squirms through gaps and holes in the wall
as he makes people quiver in the cold and says,
'I wish I was real.'

Natasha Palmer (12)
Sir Thomas Picton School, Haverfordwest

A Scary Poem

A haunted house and three teenagers

'Go in!' one said, 'I dare you!'
The three go in and the door mysteriously closes
                                       behind them,
They hear a creak upstairs, they go up and see,
The creak curiously continues, so they follow.
It lures them into a room and the door slams
                               behind them - *Slam*!
All that's in the room is a broken window and a table
                                      with a lit candle on it.
They head for the door, they turn the handle and it's locked.

They turn to the window and see outside there is a tall
Tree swaying in the wind,
One branch pushing against the window frame.
The only light comes from the flickering candle,
The house is quiet, deadly quiet.

One at a time, they start climbing out of the window,
Onto the branch of the tree,
The first two get down safely,
But the third slips and falls,
His leg gets stuck in a forked branch
And he hangs there upside down in the darkness.

Upside down, he looks up at the window,
And there is a dark hooded face staring down at him,
He untangles his leg and falls to the ground, gasping in terror.

The three run from the house, screaming with fright.

Andrew Theobald (13)
Sir Thomas Picton School, Haverfordwest

Me!

I am a tall big lad,
Never sad,
I have spiky hair,
I like eating the cold pear,
I play lots of sports,
I am the king of the tennis courts,
I have large feet,
I am very neat,
I live in the countryside,
I play football, rather 5 a side,
Living outside of Haverfordwest,
I think it is the best,
I have lots of friends out there,
But never seen a bear,
I would like to see one,
Before they are all shot by a gun,
And that's me,
The best you will ever see.

Matthew Clark (13)
Sir Thomas Picton School, Haverfordwest

The Wind

The wind,
Fiercely it runs,
Fingertips touching everything,
Arms wide,
Standing up tall,
Blowing happily,
Squirms around the corner,
Searching, seeking,
Dancing around, darting around,
Blowing happily past everything,
And every house,
Freezing cold,
The wind quivers around.

Kayleigh Turner (12)
Sir Thomas Picton School, Haverfordwest

World War Panic

My house has been bombed,
All I can see around me,
Is gravel and mess,
Around me are people,
Like mice running from a cat.

All I can hear is screaming,
My house fell down, a big crash,
I hear bombs going off,
With a bang and a crash,
My house is just bridges and wood,
Everything is destroyed,
I feel the ground shake underneath my feet,
And the rain starting to fall,
No shelter, no home.

I feel so afraid and worried, dismayed,
I worry about the rest of my family, are they OK?
My thoughts were of dying, not a happy thought in my head,
I feel nothing is left,
My dog is dead.

What is going to happen next?
War is like a horror film,
No more pain, no more war,
Can't stand the drumming in my ears,
Of the guns and bombs,
So please stop war,
I can't stand it any more.

Daisy Lewis (12)
Sir Thomas Picton School, Haverfordwest

The Haunted House

He is all alone, he approaches the dark and gloomy
Haunted house, it's pitch-black.
All he can hear is leaves crunching beneath his feet
And the wolves howling,
There is a full moon in the sky.

He walks up the unstable steps,
And knocks on the door, *knock, knock*,
No one answers, he knocks again,
He could hear a scurry, it made him jump,
And then he saw a shadow, he ran outside as fast as he could.

The wind howled through the cracks in the wall,
Loudly, he took a few steps back,
The moonlit window shows a white figure staring back at him,
He runs and never returns.

Lindsay Collins (13)
Sir Thomas Picton School, Haverfordwest

Bonfire Night Poem

Everybody's here watching the bonfire burn,
The rules of Bonfire Night they should learn,
People are giggling and playing too,
They're all going wow! and they're all going ooh!

Multicoloured lights whizzing through the air,
The excitement and the banging, we just cannot bare,
You can tell everyone here is having fun,
Eating sausages in a bun.

They're all watching these colourful lights,
Banging and fizzing all through the night,
Crackling, sparkling, banging and whizzing,
There goes another one burning and fizzing.

Laura Venables (12)
Sir Thomas Picton School, Haverfordwest

World War II!

Suddenly I heard a crash,
And a bash,
And a boom,
And a zoom,
Everything flashed before my eyes.

All I could see was a house full of rubble,
I was going to pick up my phone,
To call my mother because her house had been bombed,
All I was thinking about was what I was going to do?
I stared down at the floor and I saw Bengy,
My long-lost dog,
There was a pile of rubble on top of him!

Suddenly all I could hear was people screaming
And shouting, 'Fire, fire!'
I ran outside and I saw everybody pointing at my mother's house,
It was on fire, I had to get over there,
Because my mother was in a wheelchair,
I ran over there and they wouldn't let me in,
I said, 'My mother is in there!'

That was the last time I ever saw my mother again!
Now I'm 82 years old and I haven't seen my mother in 34 years.
I don't even have any pictures, they were all wrecked
When my house was bombed,
Not long after my mother's house was bombed.

Amy Rossiter (12)
Sir Thomas Picton School, Haverfordwest

Bluebells - Haiku

Beautiful bluebells,
Always blooming in a year
Until they are plucked.

Shreshta Musale (11)
Sir Thomas Picton School, Haverfordwest

The Haunted House

I'm inside the haunted house,
I hear a little mouse,
I see a full moon,
And the back door goes boom.

I hear shrieks of terror,
I see a wolf, what a horror,
I can hear owls outside,
I can see the black tide.

I tap on the wall,
And it echoes in the hall,
I see a hooded figure,
It is the Grim Reaper.

I hear a storm,
A new bat is born,
A shadow appears,
While a ghost hears.

Hannah Ainsworth (13)
Sir Thomas Picton School, Haverfordwest

Haunted House

The clouds covered the moon and it went dark,
I was walking down the street as the street light flickered,
I stood in front of the house and looked at it with a fright,
I walked up the path and opened the door,
I walked into the house and it was pitch-black,
The wind screamed in the dark,
The hairs on the back of my neck stood up,
The tap in the kitchen was dripping continuously,
As I went up the stairs, they creaked,
The chains clanged together,
And then the doorbell rang, and the door slammed shut!

Amy John (13)
Sir Thomas Picton School, Haverfordwest

I Hate War!

I see planes overhead,
I see people lying dead,
I see tears in people's eyes,
I see relief they're still alive,
I see *war!*

I hear cries all around,
I feel shaking in the ground,
I hear the air siren,
I feel vibration when the guns are firing,
I hear and feel *war!*

I am thinking I shall not yield,
I'm glad I'm not on the battlefield,
I am thinking, *this war is insane,*
I'm hoping this never happens again,
I am thinking and feeling *war!*

What will all this killing have achieved?
Who will help the lonely and bereaved?
How will we all survive?
When we endanger people's lives?
What is the point of *war!*

War's as evil as the Devil himself,
The stupidity of losing money and wealth,
The crying and dying, like the angel of death travelling,
We can see all our lives unravelling,
I hate war!

Matthew Western (12)
Sir Thomas Picton School, Haverfordwest

The Four Seasons

I'm when animals come out and breed,
I'm when leaves appear on trees,
I'm when daffodils come out from seed.
My season is spring.

I'm when school ends and holidays begin,
I'm when sun shines,
I'm when skies are clear and no one's in hiding.
My season is summer.

I'm when weather grows cool,
I'm when animals hibernate or migrate,
I'm when you go back to school.
My season is autumn.

I'm when the weather's at its coldest,
I'm when skies are grey,
I'm when you'll have snow if you're at your luckiest.
My season is winter.

Angharad Barnes (12)
Sir Thomas Picton School, Haverfordwest

I Like

I like
The smell of a freshly brewed tea
Waiting for me!

The smell of a cool ice cream,
Just like a dream!

The smell of hot apple pudding,
The rich smell of custard flooding!

The smell of coffee freshly ground,
Or the smell of onions, fried and browned!

The smell of everything
In summer and spring.

Samuel Williams (11)
Sir Thomas Picton School, Haverfordwest

The Battlefield

Walking home from the battlefield,
Left, right, left, right,
It's good to be going home,
And no longer having to fight,
I can still see unexploded bombs,
And men, who have fallen to the ground.
They are as still as wood left to rot,
And there is death all around.

During the battle I heard,
The scream of my mate Phil,
As he fell to the floor,
And soon became still.
I felt the tug of my heart,
As I looked at his face.
The look of shock still lingered,
But it disappeared with some pace.

I thought I would not rest,
Until justice had been done,
But then *bang* a bomb went off,
And I had to run,
I felt shocked,
As the bomb was quite near,
It was as loud as a giant shouting,
All I felt was fear.

I was enraged that the war had started,
And that people's lives were lost,
Husbands, sons, fathers,
They all died at a high cost,
When the war finally ended,
There were cheers all around,
Hitler had been defeated,
But many bodies still lie, unfound.

Holly Pretious (12)
Sir Thomas Picton School, Haverfordwest

Why Did We Have To Have This War?

Here I stand,
The howling wind blowing in my face,
As I stand here staring,
At the fire,
Glowing as hot as the sun,
Why did we have to have this war?

I can hear the burning rubble crackling,
The dogs down the road howling,
The ambulance siren in the distance,
I felt a cold shiver trickling down my spine,
The tear rolling down my cheek as slow as a snail,
Why did we have to have this war?

My family were in there, all four of them,
I feel gloomy, depressed and very scared,
They were the closest things to me,
Why us? We were all so happy,
I feel sick. All I want to do is cry. But I can't.
Why did we have to have this war?

Where will I go? Where do I stay?
I can't go to my auntie's. She's too far away.
I can't go to my friend's. She's going to her grandparents',
I could always stay here but that's too dangerous,
I'll just keep walking till I find somewhere,
Why did we have to have this war?

Hannah Rolfe (12)
Sir Thomas Picton School, Haverfordwest

My Mum

My mum is beautiful,
My mum is clever,
My mum will be there for ever and ever.
My mum is lovely, cuddly and warm,
My mum will make sure I come to no harm.

I love my mum!

Chris Williams
Sir Thomas Picton School, Haverfordwest

Welsh Dragon

Welsh dragon is intense,
With its red spiky tongue,
Flies the skies in peace,
Never to be disturbed,
It's almighty claws are ready,
Its wings as fierce as a tiger,
The coat shining red,
Eyes like a snake,
Looking after Wales with all its got,
Hunting predators from all directions,
Sitting up in the sky to show his pride,
Its swirly long tail will stick up until the world ends!
Protects Wales when everyone's asleep,
Bulging muscles like a bowling ball,
Ready for anything coming our way!

Oliver Reyland (13)
Sir Thomas Picton School, Haverfordwest

Blazing Red

Red is a sunset
Blazing and bright
Red is feeling bright and brave
With all your might.

Red is a sun burn
A spot on your nose
Sometimes red
Is a red, red rose
Just like a pimple on your toes.

Red is hot
Just like my sister's smelly socks
The large big flame blazing and bright
Lighting up the big starry night.

Jordan Beavis (11)
Sir Thomas Picton School, Haverfordwest

Nazi Attack

I saw tanks shooting rockets,
I then heard our base being blown up,
The Nazi planes going over our trench,
Then we saw the French,
I then saw our plane was dropping bombs on the tanks.

I heard the explosion come from guns,
I can feel the ground shake like an earthquake,
The tanks are getting closer,
The bangs are getting louder,
The army started to scream in pain like a baby.

I keep on thinking, *I'm going to die,*
I'm feeling frightened and scared,
My squad were all thinking of a nice meal,
Everyone that isn't real,
The noise came nearer.

Then I had to take action,
I shot my gun as fast as I could,
The bullets zoomed past,
Then the noise got closer,
The tank fired *bang* and it hit me.

Joshua Lee (12)
Sir Thomas Picton School, Haverfordwest

Our Mummy

Our mummy, the biggest diamond of them all
She is as soft as a beach ball
She loves us much, she is soft to touch,
We are very grateful for all that she has done,
And when we are feeling lonely, she has always come
We will love her for evermore,
Even we have a crooked door,
Our mummy!

Sarah James (11)
Sir Thomas Picton School, Haverfordwest

Best Friends

They cheer you up when
You are down,
They make you laugh,
They make you frown.

They make you happy,
They make you sad,
They make you feel
Really bad.

They'll be your strength if you are weak,
They'll be your voice if you couldn't speak,
They'll be your eyes if you couldn't see,
They'll be there when you want them to be.

Don't give up your
Friends for anything,
Boys, girls or even Cupid.

Laura Hill (13)
Sir Thomas Picton School, Haverfordwest

My Unusual Friend

My friend is an unusual friend,
His eyes are yellow and his ears bend,

One hand is blue, the other is white,
And if you ask me, I'll say that's not right.

His mum is an elephant, his dad is a wagon,
His house is a saucer and his car is a dragon.

All the kids tease him and that is not nice,
He uses his powers to turn them to mice.

His pet is a Martian and he eats everything,
But the weird thing about the Martian is that he can sing.

That's the story of my unusual friend,
Which is the one that'll never ever end!

James Riddiford (11)
Sir Thomas Picton School, Haverfordwest

Negro

Pushing, pulling, hitting, kicking,
I fight for my freedom
Against the pale coloured,
I am always left out.

I stand in the corner,
Playing in the dust,
It leaves a light brown colour
On my torn and wretched clothes.

Then I am shadowed from the blistering heat
By the muscular body of the school bully.
The torture ahead is indescribable,
Mama will not be happy.

When I arrive home,
Mama is knitting in her rocking chair,
Her head lifts, but then lowers with a sigh,
I am battered and bruised,
I am Negro.

Gavin Thomas (13)
Sir Thomas Picton School, Haverfordwest

My Week

On Monday I made my Mother's Day card,
On Tuesday I saw the table tennis team playing
                              on a trampoline,
On Wednesday I walked to a washing machine
                              from a waterfall,
On Thursday I saw a tattoo man covered in tarantulas in a tornado,
On Friday I saw a flying, flapping flamingo,
On Saturday I saw a silver singing slimy snake
                              smiling in South Africa,
On Sunday I saw a skipping snail slowly going to
                              the supermarket.

Anastasia Pashen (11)
Sir Thomas Picton School, Haverfordwest

That's What War Is

I am on the front
Death, rubble, guns, blood, that is the war,
My comrades run and shunt,
As I grow poor,
Tanks, explosions and broken bombs, that's what war is.

I am in the war fighting for a cause,
Discomfort, screaming, misery, pain, that is the war,
There is no pause,
While my flesh is burned raw,
Planes, injury, the broken floor, that's what war is.

I am hiding in a trench,
Fear, pain, worry, and more, that is the war,
I have nothing but my friends and a foldable bench,
But at least I don't have to bother with law,
Bangs and booms sounding in my heart that's what war is.

I am lying on the floor hit in the leg,
Life is cheap, it's nothing unlike the war,
They've strapped my leg to a splint and a peg,
I can still kill, so to them I am something,
Evil, evil, evil, is that the war?

Kai Lumber (12)
Sir Thomas Picton School, Haverfordwest

Spooky House

The outside of the house was scary,
Disturbing and supernatural,
The inside of the house is hair-raising,
Chilling and eerie,
In the house I heard an alarming,
Terrifying and mad noise.

Emma Tilley (14)
Sir Thomas Picton School, Haverfordwest

The Terrible War

All I can see is just black,
No lights in any of the houses,
When I look out the window,
All I can see is planes flying around like wasps,
And my dad going out for war.

Then, a bomb dropped, *bang!*
My house turned and tumbled,
A tear came to my eye,
My brother's teddy being cuddled,
So tight he was scared.

I'm scared,
I admit that,
Seeing everybody is making me think,
Of my life,
Just writing this poem is making me sad.

We're in the bomb shelter,
It's cold like ice,
Can't wait to get out of here,
All I can hear is guns, it's driving me nuts,
And all the bombs dropping from the sky,
Whoosh, they're coming down.

Don't know what we're going to do
When we get out of here,
Will we move away from all our family?
Is my dad going to live?

Cassey Bicknell (12)
Sir Thomas Picton School, Haverfordwest

Because You're Different!

When I get home,
It's dark at night,
I'm bruised and bloody
From my fight.
Can someone help me please?

No! Because you're different!

In the street,
I have to sleep,
But I can't get any,
Not a peep!
People point
And give me dirty looks,
Can't anyone read me like a book?

No! Because you're different!

When I go to the pub,
I ask for a drink,
You've got no chance,
That's what they think.
Can't you just leave me alone?

No! Because you're different!

Then they would hit me
In the face!
Why can't I just sink
Without a trace?

Because I'm different,
Because I'm black!

Stewart Coombes (13)
Sir Thomas Picton School, Haverfordwest

Peace No More

As I went to the park with my friends,
The world was coming to an end,
Bang! Boom! The bombs went off,
And everyone began to cough.

I ran and ran as fast as I could,
To get to the shelter, that would be good.
It was like a disease, through the whole world it spread,
And my mother was lying there, in her bed.

She was lying there sound asleep,
But then I began to weep and weep,
I had to protect her from the war,
Especially the bombing planes that I saw.

I ran around like a headless chicken,
As I saw the bombs that the Germans were nicking,
They were aiming at our house, shouting out loud,
If they got the right target, they would be proud.

Like my sister, I panicked and panicked,
The world was getting oh, so manic,
So what did we do to deserve this war?
We haven't got any peace no more.

Amy Davies (12)
Sir Thomas Picton School, Haverfordwest

Hedgehog

A hedgehog woke up in the spring,
Who wanted to stand up and sing,
He went to the pond of which he was fond,
And dived in with a rubber ring.

As the winter dawned the hedgehog got up,
But he was only a little pup,
He went to the snow which was very cold,
And had hot chocolate in a cup.

Ben Clague (11)
Sir Thomas Picton School, Haverfordwest

But This Is War

I can see death, people dying,
All around me mothers crying,
Houses in ruin, ardent fire,
Broken churches, no longer higher,
But this is war.

I hear bombs dropping like thunder,
I look outside and I wonder,
Why is there death and destruction?
Just because of Hitler's construction,
But this is war.

I feel dust covering my bleeding nose,
The wardens are carrying the fire hose,
A scary thought has entered my head,
If Hitler invaded, would we be dead?
But this is war.

Running away all alone,
From that place I once called home,
Chug-chug-chug, a plane flies ahead, guns firing,
Bang! Such pain, I'm tiring,
But this is war.

Darren Johns (13)
Sir Thomas Picton School, Haverfordwest

Scary Poem

The full moon sent a ghostly gleam
Upon the dark and silent stream
The mansion windows black and dark
No welcome lights just old and stark
Ghostly shadows lie unseen
Cold and lonely no longer homely
No children's voices to fill the air
Just monsters, darkness; no one there
A night for spirits, the living dead
No one dare enter, no footsteps tread.

Gareth Harries (13)
Sir Thomas Picton School, Haverfordwest

There I Was Standing

There I was
Standing there
Like a melon head
Shocked out of my brain
With rubble everywhere.

I felt someone touching me
I looked around and saw nobody
But screaming louder than fireworks
But shouting louder than the sirens
I wish it could stop.

I don't know what to do
I feel miserable
Lost
All my feelings are muddled up
I feel sad, my mum is crying.

What is going to happen?
We hear ticking of a bomb
Then hear
Boom! Boom!
I need to go
I need to go now!

Alex Kirk (12)
Sir Thomas Picton School, Haverfordwest

Fox Hunting

One frosty morning in a field,
The silence was disturbed.
A red, bushy tail swept through the grass,
Followed by a pack of screaming hounds,
The huntsman blew his horn,
The field thundered by,
A cry of hands went up, 'Gone to ground!'
But that crafty fox, he
Bolted and lived another day.

Thomas Glover (12)
Sir Thomas Picton School, Haverfordwest

World War II

I can still see it now,
The screaming of the people,
The shots of the guns,
All the crushed metal,
The light from the beaming red sun.

I can still hear it now,
The landing of the bombs,
Bits of metal getting flung,
I see splinters off the wood,
And fathers at battle with their sons.

I was standing there thinking,
Of what was going to happen next,
I heard the chugging of the planes,
Bits of cloth covered with bloodstains,
The wind as cold as frozen ice,
That has been in your freezer night after night.

I felt frozen still standing there,
The squeaking of the cannon wheels,
I felt everyone's fear,
I was sure we were going to win,
Beat the Germans at their very last limb,
I hated the war.

Christina Cunliffe (12)
Sir Thomas Picton School, Haverfordwest

All About Rugby

Cardiff Blues are really cool
But not as cool as Scarlets.
I sit and dream about them
When I'm by the pool.

I think about the day
I would like to play for my
Favourite team of all,
Scarlets, Scarlets, Scarlets.

Andrew Lamport (11)
Sir Thomas Picton School, Haverfordwest

Look What's Happening!

On my way home from school,
There was German bombers hiding in my pool,
I ran to my shelter to be protected,
So hopefully I wouldn't be affected,
I sat and waited in suspense,
My feelings were getting very intense.

I felt a shiver down my spine,
Just like the time I tasted wine,
I heard a great big *boom* and a *bang,*
The noise was as sharp as vampire's fangs!
I saw a baby crying out loud,
I thought I was lost amongst this entire crowd.

There's a strange and peculiar smell lingering in the air,
But not many people could actually care,
My heart was racing faster than ever,
All I could hear was 'Has anyone seen Trevor?'
I turned around and stopped and stared,
My house had suddenly disappeared,
I wondered why my house had gone,
But then I saw a gone off bomb.

These vandals are not going to get away with this,
If only I could be granted with a wish,
Then I would stop all this silliness about the war,
And call it quits, no one won, it was a draw!

Tania Hancock (12)
Sir Thomas Picton School, Haverfordwest

The War

The war is an awful place,
I can see someone getting shot in the face,
I can see my friend on the ground,
No longer making a sound,
I can see someone aiming at me,
Bang! They shot me in my knee.

The war should not be allowed,
I see someone shouting in a crowd,
I felt so sad,
When I shot this poor old lad,
When I saw someone die,
I just wanted to cry.

The war is like a battlefield,
Where no one has a shield,
I wish I was with my wife,
As I am out here risking my life,
I thought I was dead,
But it missed me, 3 inches from my head.

The war is so crazy,
I see no flowers, no daisy,
Now this is the end,
I wish I could stay here with my friend,
I wish I could tell my family goodbye,
Because I know I am going to die.

Jessie Jones (12)
Sir Thomas Picton School, Haverfordwest

The Sounds Of The War

Bang, I hear a bomb drop,
Bang, a house fell down,
Bang, is all I heard all night,
Bang, an explosion in town,
Bang.

Knock, a knock at my door,
Knock, I release the lever,
Knock, I open the door really wide,
Knock, I'm told to leave,
Knock.

Boom, another bomb drops,
Boom, I hear a tumble,
Boom, it was as loud as a blasting radio,
Boom, then I hear a rumble,
Boom!

Bang, knock and *boom,*
The sounds of the war,
Noises in the air like flies,
Explosions were all I saw.

Bang, knock and *boom!*

Joanne Griffiths (12)
Sir Thomas Picton School, Haverfordwest

War

War is frightening,
War is dangerous,
War is fun and noisy,
War sees food rations,
War feels fear,
War smells of death,
War is no more.

Sam Stayner (12)
Sir Thomas Picton School, Haverfordwest

Running To The Shelter

I saw a bomb and I started to run,
All I could see were guns, guns, guns,
I headed to the shelter but I fell in a ditch and I
Had a big, big stitch.

I tried to climb out,
And I heard a shout,
I got out again,
And I ran to find out,
All I found was a bloody floor.

So I ran to the shelter,
And opened the door,
A big bomb appeared,
I jumped on the floor,
My hands on my head,
Then I felt like I was dead.

Chris Chan (12)
Sir Thomas Picton School, Haverfordwest

World War II

I was walking on the street when I heard a bomb drop,
It sounded like a really loud boom!
Then I saw a woman screaming in the room,
Then,
Boom!

I carried on walking along,
When I saw a baby cry,
And I said, 'I cannot fly,'
The baby was as loud as a football crowd.

Then I heard lots of gunshots and then I
Knew I was being shot at,
He was very fat, he had a fat cat with a hat.

Josey Protheroe (12)
Sir Thomas Picton School, Haverfordwest

Why?

Why do we always get picked on?
They always call us names,
They racially abuse us,
And say we're not the same,
It's not fair!
Why?

Why do we get the old things?
They always get the new,
They don't seem to understand
That we have feelings too.
It's not fair!
Why?

Why do they think they are better than us?
We should be treated right,
We are only a different colour,
We're dark and they're light,
It's not fair!
Why?

What have we ever done to them?
They hurt and make us sad,
They never seem to leave us alone,
They shout and say we're bad,
Why can't they stop?
Why won't they stop?
Why don't they stop?
It's not fair!
Why?

Holly Richards (13)
Sir Thomas Picton School, Haverfordwest

Wartime

I see bombs,
I see guns,
I see people eating buns,
I see children like men,
I see birds like planes,
I see blood and bursting brains.

I heard bangs,
I felt cold,
I saw soldiers being bold,
I heard chugs,
I felt dry,
I saw children about to cry.

I felt hungry,
I didn't feel clean,
I thought the Germans were really, really mean,
I felt so lonely,
I felt so sad,
The German killers are making me mad.

I knew I was bold,
I knew I would die,
I knew I was about to say goodbye,
I knew people's feelings,
I knew lots of friends,
I knew life and war was coming to an end.

Anthony Yau (12)
Sir Thomas Picton School, Haverfordwest

Why Me?

I may be different
but I don't deserve this,

Teased, taunted and bullied,
I'm the only one.

Ignored, abused, afraid,
no one will ever understand.

Alone, tired, independent,
no one will help me.

Why me?

Why me?

Sad, miserable, down,
they know nothing . . .
nothing at all.

Robyn Fisher (13)
Sir Thomas Picton School, Haverfordwest

The House

As we walked up to the house,
We heard a squeal of a fieldmouse,
Shall we go inside
Or shall we run and hide?
As we went in,
Both of us tripped over a bin,
In the bin was a dead cat,
Lying next to a dead bat,
As we heard the floorboards creak,
We heard the fieldmouse squeak,
With a big slam of the door,
We heard the fieldmouse no more.

Curtis Elliott (13)
Sir Thomas Picton School, Haverfordwest

Revenge
(Based on 'Roll of Thunder, Hear my Cry!' by Mildred D Taylor)

Hear comes the bus,
Ready to soak us,
They hate us 'cause they're white,
But this time we'll stand and fight!

So Stacey hatched a brilliant plan,
To get revenge as soon as we can.
We'll dig a ditch to make them capsize,
Make it big and just the right size.

Off to work we went,
We grabbed four plates and a few buckets with dents,
Stacey told us to dig in the road,
Little man got dirty but did as he was told.

After the hole was done,
We went back to school and had to run,
Covered to the knees in mud caked on thick,
The horrible red mud was the colour of a brick.

We leapt out of school as soon as the bell rang,
To see our work as fast as we can.
We were so shocked, as much to our surprise,
The hole had grown and doubled in size!

We dive into the hedge to hide for a bit,
Until the bus comes, quietly we will sit.
We wait with silent, tense nerves,
And wait for the bus to come round the curves.

The bus comes hurtling towards us,
Little man is dirty but too excited to fuss,
The bus plummets right into our lake,
The driver is so mad he begins to shake!

Now that we've had our revenge,
We've shown we'll fight until the bitter end!

Danielle Jones (13)
Sir Thomas Picton School, Haverfordwest

Grim

It was sunset,
The two kids stood at the gates,
They looked up and down the street,
To see if anyone was watching,
They then jumped over the gates,
It went dark and it began to rain.
The two kids looked puzzled at each other
And went on.
They looked at the house.
It was severely worn down,
Slates were hanging and the path was covered in brambles,
Yet it was the best way in,
They made their way to the dark door,
As they walked towards the door, the street lamps began to fade,
They knocked on the door
And began to laugh
But they soon stopped when it opened,
They enter the house and lit up their torches.
As they did the room was flooded with lights
As candles went up all around the room,
The kids looked up at the stairs and saw a figure,
It came into the light and said,
'Your days are numbered,'
They then realised it was a haunted house.

Gareth Bateman (13)
Sir Thomas Picton School, Haverfordwest

The Plan

He handed me a shovel with a strange look in his eye,
The kind of look that would make some little children cry,
A look of fear, a look of hate, a look of satisfaction,
In a way and in a sense, I had the same reaction.
We went outside and looked across, the children in the rain,
We felt the same we are the same and we could feel their pain,
This plan was harsh, this plan was cruel, this plan was inhumane,
But all of us would risk it, we'd try it, were all of us insane?

We ran up the road to victory, we ran up the slippery path,
But all of us wondered, yes they should face our wrath,
We slipped and tumbled, and stumbled and fell,
But we had to finish this before the last bell,
We ran on and on, we had to get there quickly,
I accidentally swallowed some mud, it tasted so sickly,
Some fell down but still went on, we were soldiers heading into a war,
I had headaches, colds, pains and struggles, my feet were so sore!

The forest had eyes, it was staring, it could see,
It was terrifying, it looked at us cautiously,
We ran past the crossroads and on for a bit,
We came to a halt, the plan, this was it.
We stared at each other and then at the mud,
It looked so disgusting, it was dirty sud,
Stacey took a shovel and held it above the earth,
He smiled as he pushed the blade in, it was all the worth.

Owain Glyn Evans (13)
Sir Thomas Picton School, Haverfordwest

Black And White

Laughed at in the shops,
Thrown out of clubs,
Abused by the cops,
Not served in pubs.

There is a fight,
Who will win?
Black and white,
What a sin.

Graffiti on the wall,
Another racist comment,
Who will break our fall,
Through all this torment?

A quiet life
Is all we need,
No struggle, no strife,
Just equality, we plead.

Carl Rees (13)
Sir Thomas Picton School, Haverfordwest

Dogs!

Dogs can be small,
Dogs can be fat,
Dogs can be tall,
Not the size of a rat,
Dogs can be loud,
Dogs can be quiet,
And if I'm honest with you,
My dog runs riot,
I like dogs,
However big or small,
I like dogs,
I like them all.

Tess Bamber (11)
Sir Thomas Picton School, Haverfordwest

Black And White

It started many years ago,
that's when the prejudice began.
When the whites ventured into Africa,
to explore that unknown land.
They shot, killed and dragged them away
to a place they'd never been,
to be slaves in all America,
to be kept like animals;
never to be free!

But when the slavery was banned,
the hate did not stop then.
It carried on for all these years,
hatred, misery, depression and doubt;
take hold and don't let go.
Until they have been hurt
in a pain you'll never know.

But you will see every one of you,
that equality is good and true.

And they will have their justice,
they'll see one day,
the tables will turn the other way,
it will be black and white,
not white and black.

And they will have their justice,
they'll see one day,
the tables will turn the other way,
it will be happiness and love,
not sadness and hate.

And then we will all be truly great!

Sara Williams (13)
Sir Thomas Picton School, Haverfordwest

Imagine

Imagine a world
where we are all the same.
We have no differences and
life is not a dirty game.

Imagine a world
where there is one religion.
We all get along and
there is no competition.

Imagine a world
where there is no race.
We are all the same colour on
our body and on our face.

Imagine a world
where we are one.
No abusing, no fighting,
no battles to be won.

Imagine a world,
I can, can you?

William Denham (14)
Sir Thomas Picton School, Haverfordwest

Prejudice

P eople waiting around the corner to laugh and make fun.
R egret going outside - just get mocked.
E verybody laughs. It feels like the whole world laughs.
J okes and names, taunts and sneers.
U pset, miserable and depressed.
D on't have any friends.
I want to hide myself away.
C ruel people make my life a misery.
E very morning I wake up sad.

Ashley Williams (13)
Sir Thomas Picton School, Haverfordwest

A Best Friend for Life

If your best friend is like my best friend then,
She is a best friend for life.

If you tell her all your secrets and compare
each other's gossip then,
She is a best friend for life.

If she is your strength when you are weak,
your voice when you cannot speak then,
She is a best friend for life.

If her grass is always greener
and she makes you laugh then,
She is a best friend for life.

If you share the same opinions
and share each other's wardrobe then,
She is a best friend for life.

So if your best friend is like my best friend
then you definitely,
Positively
Have a best friend for life.

Ruby Rone (13)
Sir Thomas Picton School, Haverfordwest

Prejudice

P eople pick on me,
R acism is the problem,
E very day I get up, I fear being bullied
J ust because I'm a different colour,
U gly, that's what they call me,
D irty, scruffy, anything,
I 'm isolated from other children,
C riticised for the way I am,
E very day I'm treated like this, that's just me and that's my life.

Sophie Raymond (13)
Sir Thomas Picton School, Haverfordwest

Brothers And Sisters

It's funny the way
you always argue.

But when you're apart
you always worry.

And you wait cautiously till they're back
and argue! Argue! Argue!

But it comes as a shock
when they don't come back.

And you wonder at night
if they will or not.

But when they don't,
you wonder why.

And you have to ask,
'Is it because of I?'

Callum Griffiths (12)
Sir Thomas Picton School, Haverfordwest

Friendship!

Our friendship can't be broken,
No matter how hard you try.
We'll be friends for evermore,
And never say goodbye.

You're always there to help me,
In wind or rain or shine.
I'm always there for you as well,
Any place, any time.

If you ever need me,
I'm right there by your side
Like the mighty powerful bond
Of the ocean and the tide.

Nicola Tatton (12)
Sir Thomas Picton School, Haverfordwest

It Isn't Fun

You make me feel
    Dejected,
        Depressed
            and down.

You do it for fun,
You make me feel
    Lonely,
        Lost
            and low.

You do it for fun,
But do you?
Do you do it for fun?
Are you just sad and have no one?
Because I know how it feels . . .
. . . *and it isn't fun!*

Nikita Lewis (13)
Sir Thomas Picton School, Haverfordwest

The Fox

Those sharp, beady eyes,
That long, white-tipped tail,
Catching its prey,
Without fail.

That strong, sharp jaw,
Gobbling its food
With the help of its claw,
Not leaving a straw.

He strikes his pose,
And watches you,
Then with a pounce,
He . . . gobbles you!

Hina Bagha (13)
Sir Thomas Picton School, Haverfordwest

Some Of Us

Some of us are white,
Some of us are black,
Some of us are picked on
Because we are black.

Some of us are tall,
Some of us are small,
Some of us are picked on
Because of our height
And because we are black.

Some of us are fat,
Some of us are thin,
Some of us are picked on
Because of our weight
And because we are black.

All of us are different
In our own special way,
But why should we be picked on
Because of our colour,
Height or weight?
But why?
We are all human.

Michael Watts (13)
Sir Thomas Picton School, Haverfordwest

People

P eople say the most horrible things about
R ace, religion and background and
E verything and anything,
J ust because they can.
U nkindness is all around us,
D estroying friendships and families,
 I ncapable of liking people for who they really are, these people,
C ruel and nasty, why don't they realise that
E veryone's the same. Aren't they?

Yasmin Nur (13)
Sir Thomas Picton School, Haverfordwest

We Are The Same

We are the same,
Two ears, two hands.
Two feet, two eyes,
One mouth.
But are we accepted?
No, we are not,
And all because we are black.

We are the same,
We laugh, we cry.
We bleed and hurt and play,
But are we accepted?
No, we are not,
And all because we are black.

We are the same,
We sleep, we grow.
We live, we love, we die,
But we will never be accepted
Whatever we do,
And all because we are black.

Becci Rees (13)
Sir Thomas Picton School, Haverfordwest

Eagles

Eagles can see all around,
Searching for their prey,
Talons poised, beak sharpened for grabbing their prey,
Feathers rustling in the wind, still searching for their prey.
Then the eagle spots something moving on the ground,
He suddenly hurtles to the ground.
Smack!
The prey is in his grasp.
After the carcass is stripped bare,
He flies back into the wind,
Feathers rustling, without a care in the world.

Adam Sharp (12)
Sir Thomas Picton School, Haverfordwest

My Imagination

Snow is a big, white blanket covering the ground,
Red is the sunset,
Peace is a dove,
Scoring is the thrill of the game,
My baby brother's cheeks are the softest thing you can ever get.
Wheels are spinning discs on the motorway,
Spiders' legs are like a plunger on a wall,
Dogs' noses are like wet pieces of coal,
Trains' steam is like a cloud in the sky,
Hallowe'en masks are like a bad nightmare,
Angels are all the love in the world,
Goosebumps are like running spikes,
Glory is a gold medal,
Bubbles in a bath are like froth in a pop bottle.

Kern Cunningham (11)
Sir Thomas Picton School, Haverfordwest

Stare

Why do they stop and stare?
The nightmare.
Why is it always me
Who makes everyone run and flee?

I roll down the street,
Head in my hands, scuffing my feet,
No new people to meet.

Just because I may not look the same,
I still feel like I am the one to blame,
It's the wheelchair they see, then me.

This is my life with a disability,
What is wrong with me?

Kate Lewis (13)
Sir Thomas Picton School, Haverfordwest

The Dragon

The dragon is a fire-breathing creature,
A human-gobbling creature,
It lies in wait behind tree and stone,
And gobbles them up including the bone.

A dragon is sometimes a hungry creature,
A red or green, greedy creature,
It swallows young girls and young boys,
Even whole families including their toys.

The dragon is a fearsome creature,
A scaly, jewel-encrusted, winged creature.
A fierce thing feared by all,
Everyone is glad to see it fall.

Not true!

The dragon is a gentle creature,
A caring, sharing, lucky creature,
Who protects our land and shares his heart
And gives us strength to do our part.

Victoria Squire (13)
Sir Thomas Picton School, Haverfordwest

War

War is a terrible thing,
With guns and tanks and everything.

The men might fight bravely,
But they are too scared to be in the navy.

Everything is terrible to see,
And all the people are sad.

Loved ones have gone to fight,
But they may never come back in sight.

Do you have to fight?
Why can't you just be happy,
Not sad!

William Squire (11)
Sir Thomas Picton School, Haverfordwest

Young Writers - Great Minds From Wales Vol I

Why Am I So Different?

Why am I so different?
Why am I so left out?
And you're always so innocent,
You'll be famous without a doubt.

Why am I so hated
And so totally slated
While you are so overrated?
They all think you're so sophisticated!

While you are being educated,
I am picking cotton,
As soon as you were remembered,
I was left, forgotten.

Can you help me? What have I done?
Just because I'm a black man's son.
You pick on me, punch me, you kick me and shove me.
Why can't you just like me, or maybe even love me?

Tanya Griffiths (13)
Sir Thomas Picton School, Haverfordwest

Night Chase

Dark as a river of mud,
Dark as the night,
Running through a thicket of trees,
Running blind with fright.

I'm being chased by white people,
White as a cloud,
I don't know why they're chasing me,
But I hide in a hole in the ground.

They're chasing me through a dark forest
With torches burning bright,
I know why they are chasing me,
It's because I'm black and they're white.

Barnaby Swift (13)
Sir Thomas Picton School, Haverfordwest

Fox And Hound

The fox sped away,
The hound not far behind,
He's catching up, going
Faster and faster.

The trap is set,
There's nowhere to run,
Straight into the farm,
Ignoring the chickens,
Ignoring the rabbits,
Ignoring his hunger.

Running slower and slower,
The hound going faster and faster,
The rain is coming,
Pouring it down,
The scent is going, it's time to hide,
In the barn, he hides in the hay.
The hounds running past,
Safe for now I would say.

Siân Adams (13)
Sir Thomas Picton School, Haverfordwest

I Am

I am the invisible one,
'Who's she?' you ask,
I've been here years!
You just haven't seen me.

I am the unsuitable one,
The one always picked last,
You have excluded me,
I am your last choice.

I am the forgotten one,
Stereotyped and pitied,
Why do you hate me?
I am just like you.

Sophie Dobson (13)
Sir Thomas Picton School, Haverfordwest

Cleaning The Attic

When you clean you put things away,
When you clean you dust all day,
When you put things away,
You find an old picture astray.

Old memories come up to stay
Of parties and holidays.
All your attention goes away,
On the memories that were once astray.

Some memories are good,
Some memories are bad,
Some memories are happy,
Some memories are sad,
All the memories we find,
Nothing compares to the present time.

Hannah Griffiths (13)
Sir Thomas Picton School, Haverfordwest

Prejudice

P retending that it's okay,
R acism taints my life,
E very day a lifetime of torture,
J ust because I'm black,
U sing cruel words, insulting my background,
D o you think I'm different?
I have feelings, just as much as the next person,
C an't you see your hearts are filled with hate?
E njoying the thought of death, it must be better than this.
   Will things ever change? I'm exactly the same as you,
   Just in different coloured skin.

Siobhan O'Sullivan (13)
Sir Thomas Picton School, Haverfordwest

The Power Cut

There was a storm the other night,
Loud, cracking and crashing, it gave me a fright.
Then, all of a sudden, there was no light,
I could not see anything, I lost my sight.

Then Mum came with a candle to lighten my room,
She said, 'Don't worry, there will be light soon!'
It was as scary as a creepy, dark tomb.
I looked out of my window and there was the moon.

I started to sing a warm, comforting song,
Then, with a flicker of light, the lights came back on.
It wasn't so scary, I was wrong,
There was nothing to worry about, it wasn't off for long!

Jessica Cale (13)
Sir Thomas Picton School, Haverfordwest

Goodbye

I hope you know that I will miss you,
My heart believes that you'll miss me too.
I understand that you have to go,
And I wrote this poem to let you know
That I hope you know that I will miss you,
And my heart believes that you will miss me too.

I am glad we see each other in the holidays,
But I will miss you always.
I know our friendship will never die,
And we both know that it is not a lie.
I will say it one more time,
I will always miss you, goodbye.

Lisa Owens (12)
Sir Thomas Picton School, Haverfordwest

Why?

Why is there prejudice?
Why is someone else superior?
I haven't hurt anyone,
You think I don't have feelings,
But I do.

I'm lonely and isolated
Because you want to have fun.
I'm dejected and depressed
And you don't care.
Just because I'm black,
You think I don't have feelings,
But I do.

'It won't always be like this,'
That's what people say.
'Things will change,'
Only if someone speaks out.
Only when people realise we have feelings,
Because we do.

Catherine Owen (13)
Sir Thomas Picton School, Haverfordwest

Why Am I Not There?

I see my family
Having so much fun
Without me.
Why am I not there?

I see my friends
Playing without me.
Why am I not there?

Why am I not there
With my friends and family?
I now know because I've gone,
But why does no on come to see my grave?

Laura Rogers (11)
Sir Thomas Picton School, Haverfordwest

Why?

Why do people joke about me?
Why do they laugh and grin?
Why do they call me names?
Why do they snigger and sneer?
Why do they isolate me because of my colour?
Why do they poke fun?
Why do people want to make me feel so low?
Why can't they just leave me alone?
Why do they have to torment me?
Why?

Bethan Rees (13)
Sir Thomas Picton School, Haverfordwest

Colours

Red . . . is warm and spicy just like a tikka masala,
Orange . . . is hot, bright and alive and the colour fizzes up inside me.
Yellow . . . is sunshine related and fills my body quickly with happiness.
Blue . . . is cold, sometimes scary and it goes as high as the sky.
Green . . . is organic and is short and spiky like the long stretches of
                                        grass around the world.
Pink . . . is fantastic, vibrant and makes me me.

Purple . . . is a deep, lonely and an everlasting dying colour.

Jo Davies (12)
Sir Thomas Picton School, Haverfordwest

War Poem

This is the war happening now, in 1939,
All the planes bombing down, destroying all the towns,
Lying down on the beach thinking it's a beautiful day,
But when you see the battleships,
Then you know it is not a good time to stay.
War is very scary, some people have nowhere to live,
People fighting every day, then you say, am I going to live?

Janette Price (11)
Tregynon Hall School, Powys

Hate - Sadness

Hate is black in the dark of a cave.
Hate sounds like drums beating in the darkness.
Hate tastes like mouldy cheese with last week's milk.
Hate smells like mouldy rubbish in the back.
Hate looks like a bull charging at you.
Hate feels like rotten meat in the kitchen.
Hate reminds me of a load of rats eating meat.
Sadness is the white of a dying person's face,
Sadness sounds like the screaming person.
Sadness tastes like the bitter taste of my granny's cooking.
Sadness smells like musty old photographs of old ladies.
Sadness feels like being left on my own.
Sadness reminds me of hopes lost and a future uncertain.

Rebecca Williams (15)
Tregynon Hall School, Powys

Love

Love is a warm red,
Love sounds like the silence of the waves
Hitting the rocks at the beach,
Love tastes like lip gloss on your girlfriend's lips,
Love smells like having your girlfriend
Resting her head on your shoulder,
Love looks like sitting in a beach hut with
An angel in your arms,
Love feels like butterflies in your belly and being high as a kite
And as low as being in a boxing ring with Ali,
Love reminds me of all the hate in my life
And all the happiness in my life at the same time -
Mixed feelings.

Avion Warman (15)
Tregynon Hall School, Powys

Feelings

Happiness is the sound of children playing,
Happiness is the taste of a big Sunday lunch,
Happiness smells like the flowers of spring,
Happiness is the look of joy in people's faces,
Happiness reminds me of all the good things in life.

Sadness is the sound of crying children,
Sadness is the taste of a sour sweet in your mouth,
Sadness smells like an old junkyard,
Sadness is the look of disappointment in people's faces,
Sadness feels like the cold snow all around you,
Sadness reminds me of poverty.

Anger is the sound of shouting voices,
Anger is the taste of a burning hot curry,
Anger smells like a fire burning,
Anger is the look of frustration in people's faces,
Anger feels like a hot coal in your hand,
Anger reminds me of war.

Hunger is the sound of someone's stomach rumbling,
Hunger is the taste of what you're looking at,
Hunger smells like next door's food cooking,
Hunger is the look of starvation in people's faces,
Hunger feels like an empty pit within you,
Hunger reminds me of food.

Dave Mitchell (16)
Tregynon Hall School, Powys

Tropical Island

The trees sway in the breeze,
Coconuts fall from Heaven,
The birds sing all day,
The waves glimmer like diamonds,
The sky is like a bottomless pit,
Turtles bathe in the sand,
Dolphins jump as they're putting on an act.

Richard Nichol (14)
Tregynon Hall School, Powys

Love And Hate

Hate

Hate is the colour of red in anger,
Hate sounds like slamming door of anger,
Hate tastes like a sore mouth,
Hate smells like a red roaring fire,
Hate looks like the end of a marriage,
Hate feels like a rough carpet,
Hate reminds me of parents arguing with each other.

Love

Love is the red plumped up satin heart,
Love sounds like a couple of adults saying I do,
Love tastes like sweet and sticky treacle pudding,
Love smells like dying flowers in a vase,
Love looks like two old people hugging,
Love feels like warmth from a radiator,
Love reminds me of hugging my mum.

Matthew Pritchard (14)
Tregynon Hall School, Powys

Colours Of Life

Red is danger harsh and hot,
Black is human flesh starting to rot,
Yellow is happy light and bright,
Pink is the sky on a summer's night,
Green is tranquil calm and cool,
Brown is dull like the first day back at school,
Blue is pure, calm and clear,
Grey is dark and dingy fear,
These are the colours of life.

Callie Skelding (13)
Tregynon Hall School, Powys

Love

Love is the colour of red
which is left upon a warm kiss.

Love is the sound of the birds
on a summer's morning.

Love is gentle like a
newborn baby.

Love is that very smell of her
perfume on you.

Love is happiness
which is filled with excitement.

Love is strong which can't be broken.

Love is being with the one
you love,

which is my girlfriend.

Adam Rushton (15)
Tregynon Hall School, Powys

Hate

Hate is the colour of blood running down your face,
Hate is the sound of your nose breaking into a million pieces,
Hate tastes like your tongue as your teeth bite through
as if it were butter,
Hate smells like the cold wet pavement as you fall to the ground,
Hate looks like a red blanket thrust over your head enveloping
your thoughts,
Hate feels like five boulders battering you like an ant,
Hate reminds you of everyday life.

Cori Belliard (16)
Tregynon Hall School, Powys

Red

Dragon's fire, scorching hot,
Fierce danger flashes,
Blood, red, dripping,
Bellowing.

Heat bubbling ferociously,
Volcano, red-hot ball of flickering fire,
Steaming, evily.

Sizzling,
Bringing hell, ruthlessly,
Burning, flames boiling,
Lava pours angrily,
Bloodshot balls fire ferociously.

Devil's evil and dangerous,
Flames come out boiling,
Red anger appears,
Steam in the air.

Katie Davies (11)
Whitchurch High School, Cardiff

Me In The Future

Trees taller than skyscrapers,
The sky red as blood,
The sun glowing down,
Trees are a baby-blue
And sea green.
All pylons touching the sky,
Houses will be triangle in any colour,
They should have different levels for cars
So there's no traffic jams.
In the future I have brown hair
With a baby-blue top as blue as the sea,
With McKenzie jeans
And Lacoste trainers,
This is me in 2000 and 33.

Aaron Elliott (13)
Whitchurch High School, Cardiff

A Colour For Me

Pink, a colour for butterflies
A colour for me.
A colour that shines,
For all to see!

Blue, a colour for winter,
A colour for a friend,
For a day of winter,
A colour that will never end!

Green, a colour for trees,
A colour for Dad,
A colour for the bees,
It won't made you *mad!*

Yellow, a colour to trust,
A colour for Mum,
That brings out Musk,
A gift for the sun!

Eve Worrell (11)
Whitchurch High School, Cardiff

Colourful Colours

Green grows everywhere,
Left, right, centre,
Leaves, grass and moss,
Calm, harmless.

Red roars like a fire,
Stops you suddenly,
Danger, danger, look out,
Loud, harmful.

Blue flows down a stream night and day,
Freezes solid while the sun glistens off,
Sound soothing your mind.

Steven Freshney (11)
Whitchurch High School, Cardiff

Vampire On The Loose

The night was dark and still,
The wind was blowing,
Then something appeared,
It was a bright light,
The window was open.

The vampire was hungry,
He went to the open window
To have a look inside.
He saw a girl, he jumped in,
She started to move,
It was a creaking sound.

The vampire jumped back,
There was a whistling sound outside
And there was a howling sound too.
The vampire went to the front door,
The creaking noise comes back.

She got up, she ran outside
To see what it was,
Something flew past her,
She ran in and locked the door,
She forgot to lock the window.

The vampire flew in the window,
The vampire was hiding,
She comes into watch telly,
She started to get cold,
She looks to see if the window was open.

She quickly locked it,
She turned on the telly,
She flicked over, a horror film came on,
She could not turn over,
All of a sudden the light went off.

She put the cover over her,
Then the vampire crept up on her,
He held her still,
Then he bit her on the neck,
She jumped up and her eyes went white.

She turned into a vampire,
They both went out
And they went to the graveyard
And they went into their gravestone
And they still lie there now.

Claire Williams (13)
Whitchurch High School, Cardiff

Red, Evil World

The flaming temper of a dragon scorching,
Molten lava oozing from a volcano,
The ferocious flames of Hell,
Creeping, burning nightmares
Seeking an evil place to lurk.

War spreads,
The Earth plunges towards the bowels of Hell,
Darkness, deceit, treachery.
Evil cavalry,
Sent forth to end the world,
Red shows this!

Roaring flames are engulfing,
The world will be no more.
Red anger seizes you,
The lair of the dragon,
The flames of the dragon
Will conquer the world.
Red is in the midst of this.

The dark side of romance,
Red roses are a gift from the heart,
Given to those whom you love.
Red shows many sides of a person's thoughts.

Harry Wootten (11)
Whitchurch High School, Cardiff

Red And Evil

Dragons' breath,
Sounds like danger,
God of war,
Kills again,
Molten lava,
Burns through Hell,
Bloodthirsty Devil,
Cackles with laughter.

Bloody murder,
Extremely violent,
God of war,
Strikes again,
Volcano blasts,
Lava pours,
World turns dark,
Dragons roam.

No love to be seen
From the goddess above,
But soon she'll come
And spread her love.

Rebecca Higgins (12)
Whitchurch High School, Cardiff

Blue Is The Colour

Blue is the colour of a cold, dark plant
And the Atlantic Ocean.

Blue is the colour of the sky
Which looks down on us.

Blue is the colour of our school uniform
Which makes us look all smart.

Blue is the colour of most of the Earth
When you look from space.

Aimee Yorke (11)
Whitchurch High School, Cardiff

In 30 Years

I look at a hill, what I remember was a hill,
It is now covered in houses, little green,
Fewer birds appear in the sky,
More insects in on the floor,
Like armies going to war.
Tall skyscrapers cover the hill,
They eat into the green belt,
Turbines cover what's left of the hill
And spoil the beauty.
Trams, it's a way to travel,
Following along a track,
Taking people with blank expressions to their destination,
Controlled from inside,
Fashion, it's quite the same,
Short, low cut, knee high,
I look in the mirror, short blonde hair,
Some lines on my face, I'm getting old.
Things are changing, so am I.

Nia Holbrook (13)
Whitchurch High School, Cardiff

White Winter

In an isolated place,
A lake frothing and bubbling.

A surprising chill beckons my face,
Frozen feelings overcome me.

Numb as an iceberg,
I take small strides walking gracefully.

My mind senses
Spiritual feelings which are calm and peaceful.

I can't stop myself,
My body feels as if I am being drifted into another world.

Hoda Ali Fahiya (11)
Whitchurch High School, Cardiff

Steaming Anger

Anger,
Like the lava rushing out of a steaming volcano,
Monstrous red anger,
Thick and evil.

Anger,
Like the Devil threatening,
Bloodshot in Hell
With fierce laughter,
Scorching.

Anger,
Evil bubbling up in a poor man's head,
Ready to pounce out and attack,
Like a dragon's breath with stinging hot fire,
Ready to knock the heart out of someone
And replace it with
Steaming hot anger.

Anger,
Soon it will spread to someone else,
Different to the person it was in,
Like a devil pouring death over us all,
Horrible steaming anger.

James Brinning (11)
Whitchurch High School, Cardiff

Nature

Those living close to nature
In solitude as peasants in the country.
The world is a field and we are born to cultivate the field,
Once we learn how to do this
We can produce everything.

> We don't realise how well we have things
> Until it's too late.
> We should open our eyes as well,
> Use our mind to enjoy nature.

Zayneb Afsar (11)
Whitchurch High School, Cardiff

Warm And Cold Colours

Blue

Blue is a cold colour,
It is like being outside on a cold and frosty morning,
It's the colour of a snowball when it is frozen,
It is the colour of a raging river through a village,
It makes people shiver because it makes you cold.

Red

Red is a really hot colour,
It reminds people of blood,
Sometimes it reminds some people of being out or being injured,
Red is the colour of blood,
Red is a danger colour, it is not very bright
And on traffic lights it means danger or stop.

Grey

Grey is the colour of the sky when it is about to rain,
Grey is not really a colour it is a shade,
Grey is the colour of mashed up ice,
It is a cold colour because it reminds people of rain and ice.

Lee Davis (11)
Whitchurch High School, Cardiff

Red

A burning fire on Christmas Day,
A volcano erupting in the distance,
Fireworks exploding in the night sky,
Blood pouring from a man who had fallen to his death,
Red sky at night, shepherds' delight,
A ruby-red diamond sparkling in the sun,
Castle Coch standing proud in the sky,
A tiger roaring with fear,
Autumn leaves falling from the tree,
The sign of danger in the air,
The colour red.

Ellis Jones (11)
Whitchurch High School, Cardiff

Slavery

Across the dusty deserts
And over the frosted sea,
Bars surround the children
Who are desperate to be free.

Bound around their wrists
Are tight and brutal chains.
The sunshine watches sadly
As their dreams wash the drains.

The colours in their mind
Once bright, begin to fade
As they sit upon their knees
And cry, in pain, for aid.

Their misery is torture,
But they make not a sound,
As one by one they fall
In silence on the ground.

Juliet Eales (12)
Whitchurch High School, Cardiff

Death

Infertile rugged landscape
Black as coal,
Broken stumps,
A ghostly cemetery swaying in the wind,
Death!

A desolate desert tossed upon the frenzied wind.
Loss of life,
Skeletons of fiends - man
Death!

Suffocated wildlife,
Impure acid, nauseating
A blanket of stench.
Death!

Stefanie Rossi (13)
Whitchurch High School, Cardiff

Future

I look into the air,
I see
A dark purple sky
And a red sun,
Then I lie down
On the hard green grass,
Like lying on spears,
A bird flies by,
Two heads,
Four legs,
Trees growing higher than before
Like they're trying to escape,
I look into the mirror,
I'm small,
Lines on my face,
I'm old.

Samantha Curtis (13)
Whitchurch High School, Cardiff

Silver

Icy silver,
Cold and crunchy,
Silent whisper,
Shimmering, shining
In the winter, stands out.

Bright silver,
Cheery, joyful,
Sparkly, fancy,
Elegant, smooth,
In the disco, stands out.

Feelingless silver,
Not dark, not light.

Megan Sawford (11)
Whitchurch High School, Cardiff

White!

Winter's chill,
Isolated she lies alone,
Frozen, fearful,
Waiting,
Footsteps crunching
Softly through the snow.

Glistening caves shone all around,
Where was she to go?
Fluffy clouds float gracefully through the sky,
Quietly, whispers are heard as the skies open and flakes fall.

Mysterious, she listens,
The snow comes to an end.

Nothing!

Bethan Davies (12)
Whitchurch High School, Cardiff

Cheese Is Good

C heese is yellow,
H ot or cold it is up to you.
E dam or Cheddar it's all the same,
E verything if you want, it's up to you.
S oggy is not nice, it looks like a lion's mane,
E at it with eggs.

I ndian cheese is just the same.
S lowly getting yellow in the oven.

G olden yellow looks so nice,
O ld mice like it too.
O verall it is just so nice,
D reaming of it day and night.

Jemma Evans (12)
Whitchurch High School, Cardiff

The Devil From Hell

The devil from Hell
Is the one I chose,
Like a volcano steaming hot,
Roaring all night is what I hate.

I come home from work,
Roses on the floor,
Comes down all sweet,
Still the god of war.

I lie awake at night,
Hoping he will change,
I want an angel as good as gold,
But now I have a devil,
A devil from Hell.

Emma Standen (11)
Whitchurch High School, Cardiff

Red

Red anger,
Scorching, bubbling,
Raging,
Roaring in my ears.

I want to scream,
Break something,
Howl,
Whip someone.

Ferocious danger,
Dragon's breath,
Fiery thunder
Through the beaming lava.

Lorna Chamberlain (11)
Whitchurch High School, Cardiff

The Silent Scream

Waterfall,
Frothing, oozing foam.
Lonely, isolated,
Sad, numb and cold.
A silent scream
Pierces through,
Cold, silver lips.
A ghost sparkling
Against the white,
It's a nothing,
A memory,
A dead frozen memory.
It walks towards
The stunned girl,
She couldn't move,
She was lost
And it would cost
Her memory and youth,
Her dead frozen youth.

Kayleigh Rees (11)
Whitchurch High School, Cardiff

Thunderous Red

Red, the dark side in all of us,
All love and care is forgotten,
The evil anger inside takes over,
Raging, ranting, thunderous red.
Blood is curdling, red-hot fire,
Shouting, screaming, booming.
Anger is seeking a victim,
Anger sent from Hell, violent, evil,
Suffocating and consuming.
Anger lies somewhere deep in all of us.

Ellis Williams
Whitchurch High School, Cardiff

That Reminds Me

A snowy, frozen night,
Empty, calm streets,
Nothing but a dim light.

Ice shining on cars
Like diamonds,
Even twinkling stars.

Cats' eyes like little light bulbs
Blending in with the dark.

I hear whispers,
But no clouds,
It is like another winter.

Snow is sloping on rooftops,
You cuddle up at bedtime
Away from frostbite.

A snowy, frozen night.

Emily Tuckwell (12)
Whitchurch High School, Cardiff

White

The empty frozen night,
Clear frozen lakes,
The polar bear
Hunts for food.
Snowflakes fall
As dawn overcomes him,
As more fish have been caught.
Mountains become clear,
Snow foxes gather,
Footprints through the snow
As dawn overcomes them.

Stacey Harris (12)
Whitchurch High School, Cardiff

Winter Chills

Winter chills,
Sparkling nights,
Ghosts haunting the woods,
Frozen frost scattered across the land,
Whistling winds howling, telling not to show the light.

Winter chills
On Christmas Day,
A white day,
Singing children, playing and laughing
All day!

Winter chills,
Clouds rushing into storms
Through the night,
Trembling tears exploding out,
The happiness stopped
In winter chills.

Sam Lomasney (12)
Whitchurch High School, Cardiff

The Future

I was wandering the street like a lost soul,
I could see the happy sky dazing straight at me,
The birds cheeping with excitement.

As I was in the future the buildings changed,
As I walk past houses I saw it was empty and lonely,
Different they look, much bigger and scarier,
The transport was now filled with computer technology.

I look like my dad at my age now,
I'm wearing dark red jumper with scary-looking trousers
With dark shoes,
I have grey hairs now sprouted on my head,
It was soon the end for me.

Sam Worrell (13)
Whitchurch High School, Cardiff

The Beautiful Game

10 o'clock on a rainy Saturday morning,
Expectations from parents and managers are high,
We stand ready and determined,
The roar goes up as the whistle blows.

10 minutes in and it's still even,
Then a moment's brilliance
And . . . bang, we're 1 ahead.

Half-time comes
As tired legs go to the manager.
The manager gives a team talk,
They get fired up
And enter the pitch again.

The opposition fight hard to get equal,
The half goes quickly
And suddenly the whistle blows.
They get a free kick
Just on the edge of the area
With 20 seconds left.
He lines up to take it,
He fires it straight at the top corner,
Our goalie gets a hand to it,
But will it be enough?
Only time will tell,
The ball is still flying close,
But not close enough,
It skims the post and goes wide.
The clock hits nought
And the final whistle goes.
We had won,
The manager congratulates us
And that's three points in the bag!

Ross Wilson (11)
Whitchurch High School, Cardiff

Poem On A Rainy School Morning

The grey clouds thicken over the schoolyard,
The rain thuds down heavily, like big pebbles,
The wind picks up and umbrellas are snatched
Out of hands and torn into the sky,
Flying around helplessly like huge Smarties.

Children scurry around the school,
Looking for cover,
Tower block stands tall and fierce
As if it were in control of the stormy,
Horrid and cold morning.

I could just about smell the warm, freshly baked pizzas
And the hot cups of chocolate,
The smell came from the tower block entrance,
Children hurried into the tower block,
Following the chocolatey smells,
As if they were in a trance.

Jade Biddlecombe (13)
Whitchurch High School, Cardiff

Air Dive

As I jump out into the air
I felt the wind rush through my hair.
My eyes go dry as I fall,
I'm scared to jump and hit the floor in case I go to hospital once more.

I open my chute and hear the sound of the poof,
I feel so small as I jump to the floor
And my ears are vibrating at that tremendous roar.

As I land on the floor my feet feel like they cannot go numb any more,
My chute gets caught on the cactus I saw on the way down to
                                                           the floor,
I hope to do this next year but I feel like I can take no more.

Ben Carey (11)
Whitchurch High School, Cardiff

Thrill Of The Chase

He dozed in the shadows calm and content . . .
Blast of the horn shatters the quiet,
He is running for his life.
Death wraiths leap out at him, eyes bulging,
Gnawing, biting, panting, wrenching,
There are dozens and only one of him.
Flame-coloured and lithe he leaps for his home,
But it's gone,
They blocked it up.
Tired now,
He runs,
Looking for holes, safe and dark,
They're all gone, all blocked up so he can't get away.
The wraiths are nearer, they won't let him rest,
Or slake his thirst in the stream.
He is exhausted, not half alive, or even a quarter,
He's just so much bone and sinew, with a feeble spark of life.
He turns,
They've got him,
They bite and rip and shred his body, blood gushing, streaming,
He dimly registers the pain,
But it no longer seems like it's his body,
It's as if he is watching it, from far away.

Sophia Gibbs (13)
Whitchurch High School, Cardiff

Winter

Winter, an immaculate bleak image,
Full of raw, brutal coldness,
Pearl-white snowflakes cascading down continuously,
Penetrating gusts of wind blowing constantly,
Crackling and sizzling of a nearby inn's log fire,
Wafts its way into the bitter wintry air.

Stephanie Regan (13)
Whitchurch High School, Cardiff

To Be With Blue

The sky with the brightness of blue,
Sends you up and away.
The clouds that you just want to grab,
Are well beyond our reach.

The sea so blue and clear,
Makes you feel like there's nothing there.
You just want to walk away,
But the sand is solid around you.

The sea and the sky
Beautiful as they sound,
There's one big bang . . .
The wildlife, you never, ever know.

Look up and down and all around,
The blue is face to face,
You want to feel part of it
But it's not as easy as it sounds.

Bethan Carr (11)
Whitchurch High School, Cardiff

Black

I call it black,
Black as death.
Black are my curtains that hang from my wall,
My cat she is the lonesome colour black.

The night sky, it is black,
Black as coal.
Her hair black and flowing like a river,
Dark and breathless.

Brutal, cruel and violent
Yet beautiful, soft and dramatic,
Who really knows her?

Naomi Morgan (13)
Whitchurch High School, Cardiff

Dawn Breaks

The dawn breaks,
The sky is filling with reds, yellows and oranges.
Say goodbye purple and blue,
The sunrise sky is beating you.
The best colour of all is the sun,
Yellow, bold and beautiful.

Then blue takes over once again
With white clouds to fill the gaps.
The sunrise sky will fade away
For now there will be blue today.

Then the night arises black as coal
With white stars to guide the way,
As a black and white movie fades away
The moon shines in grey and white
Calling back the dark black night.

Rosemary Jenkins (11)
Whitchurch High School, Cardiff

A Rose Of Love

Love grows like a rose,
Gentle, delicate,
Anger then starts to burn,
Like the fire,
Bringing never-ending hatred,
A rose blooms,
Silent and lonely,
The fire glows
As the hatred and anger
Grows stronger,
Furiously burning it encases the rose,
Love dies,
A rose withers.

Alys Aston (13)
Whitchurch High School, Cardiff

The Ironer

In a warm, relaxing room,
In a massive house,
Hissing as steam flies about.

She irons so peacefully, very neat,
Her arm, moving back, forward,
Side to side, like stroking a cat.

With her short, bushy grey hair
Are her purple trousers and T-shirt.

Her face, so happy,
Smiling, laughing, with the other person.
Corner of her eyes wrinkled, bags
From work so hard.

Green room, green eyes, as green as
Field grass freshly grown.

Tweets from birds outside,
Time flying by as the clouds do like
Fluffy candyfloss,
But she notices nothing,
So busy,
So busy.

Amy Price (13)
Whitchurch High School, Cardiff

The Colour Poem

The colour blue makes me fall for you,
The colour red makes me wish you were dead,
The colour yellow makes me so mellow,
The colour brown gets me down,
The colour green makes me oh so keen
And the colour white shines a light just to make sure everything's right.

Kyle Deek (12)
Whitchurch High School, Cardiff

A Peaceful Land

The wind is green with
Nothing but wildlife around.

The elves that are now in the autumn of their years,
The colours that they once wore now no longer full of colour.

They now have to leave their home,
Because all the world has changed,
Their cherished land no longer green
And full of colour.

Although they still have their one river,
It flows through the morning and through the night.

The voice of the river will never fade,
You will always hear the voices singing.

The voices of such happy people,
Shall never be forgotten,
That sound like bells chiming,
That chime in such a deep tone.

There is amongst all the elves
Such beauty that you or I
Could never build,
Even never see.

Helen Tucker (14)
Whitchurch High School, Cardiff

Red

The hot colour,
Where the fire spreads across the land,
There are screams,
There is noise
As the burning village is under fire,
The trees are turning to ash,
It is gone,
All gone.

Sophie Roberts (11)
Whitchurch High School, Cardiff

Colour Mixture

Blue makes me
Shiver
When I'm all
Alone.
While red makes me
Shine
With laughter and
Happiness.
Green brings hope
For peaceful lands.
Yellow is bright
But feels sweet.
Black makes you
Chill
But brings you to
Danger.

Lauren Roberts (11)
Whitchurch High School, Cardiff

Colours Of The Rainbow

The imaginary gypsies flying in the wood,
The wind whistling through the leaves,
A picnic of ham and cheese,
Children playing with Louise.

The angry cry of the bear,
The happy cry of the baby,
The excitement of the first man on the moon,
The sorrow for a dead relation.

A dance for the rain,
A smile for the sun,
A howl for the wind
And a ghost for the mist.

Steffan Howells (11)
Whitchurch High School, Cardiff

Colours

Yellow is the sun,
Bright and early.
Blue is the sea,
Deep and full.
Green is the grass,
Short and sharp.
Orange is the fire,
Hot and raging.
Grey is the ground,
Cold and hard.
White is the clouds,
Light and fluffy.
Brown is the tree trunks,
Textured and tall.
Colours are the Earth.

Rachel John (13)
Whitchurch High School, Cardiff

Red Is Like A . . .

Red is the colour of anger
Bubbling deep inside,
Ready to pop at anytime,
Ready to come alive!

Red is the colour of fire,
With its warming glow.
Red is the colour of romance.
A sign of first true love.

Red is the colour of danger,
Do you dare to pass?
Red is the colour of a rose,
Standing proud and powerful,
Upright in the grass.

Jess Leonard (11)
Whitchurch High School, Cardiff

Colours

Red

The forgotten soldiers on the battlefield,
The cries of families being lost in bomb raids,
The touch of blood when it is spilled,
The noise of stabbing knives,
The look of the Devil's eyes as they pierce skin.

Black

The smell of oil when it is spilled,
The darkness of the night as it creeps over the world,
The graves are open so the dead are free,
The look of tar when it is being poured,
The night has come and it will never leave.

White

The smell of sweet, sweet vanilla,
The touch of a fragile daisy,
The feel of crisp white snow under my feet,
The thought of flying through pure white clouds,
The scent of a fresh lily.

Danny Jones (11)
Whitchurch High School, Cardiff

Snow

There's magic out there today,
Which washes all the gloom away.

Something which brings laughter and light,
It makes all things dark, seem bright.

The patterns on this thing, are beautiful in every way,
It leaves you with nothing to say.

Sledges zoom down the hill, getting faster as they go,
There is nothing else to say, but say that this is snow.

Sophie Standen (12)
Whitchurch High School, Cardiff

The Colour Red

Red is the colour of anger, of rage,
The battle crazed warrior charging,
The uncontrollable burst of hate,
The boy being teased lashes out at his taunters,
The wounded soldier lying forgotten on the edge of death,
The blood of the innocent slain over greed.

The colour of victory, the proud leader praising his troops,
The colour of invigoration, of courage,
The timid mouse ventures out to find food,
The colour of strength, of dedication,
A monk swearing his oaths,
The colour of ultimate glory!
This is the colour *red!*

Tom Skirrow (11)
Whitchurch High School, Cardiff

Colours, All Sorts Of Colours

Blue, a circle of icy cold Antarctica
Blowing a sweet, soft melody in the shimmering, shining sun.

Yellow, a passionate circle of joy and happiness
Spinning in the dazzling sky,
Wondering who to drop by next.

Green, a delighting fragrance that sticks out
In autumn of the fresh juicy grass.

Pink, a romantic, friendly colour that
Delights you with kindness and love.

Orange, a bright, astonishing way to end the day
With the beautiful orange sunset.

Chloe Davies (11)
Whitchurch High School, Cardiff

Bright And Hot Colours

Green

Green is a calm colour,
It makes you feel calm, relaxed
And makes you think of the nice green leaves
And the forest of green.
Green is a bright warming colour,
It makes your mood feel jealous.

Red

Red is a hot colour,
It reminds people of blood and war.
Red is a nasty colour.
Red is a sign of danger and fire,
It makes your mood feel hot and your mood turn evil.

Yellow

Yellow is a really bright colour,
It makes people happy, look good
And it stands out.
It's the colour of the sun and powerful.

Menna Davies (11)
Whitchurch High School, Cardiff

Many Feelings Of Blue

Deep blue ocean glittering in the sun,
The start of winter just begun.
The clear sky shining high,
A lost walker freezing in the cold Arctic,
Icy cold water running from a cold tap,
The feeling of a day begun,
Snow falling on the ground comforting everything around.

Sarah Thomas (11)
Whitchurch High School, Cardiff

Seasons

I wake up in the morning
All I can hear is the baby birds cheep,
Cheeping in the bush where their nest is
And the birds are calling,
Calling to their mum asking for food.
I wake up in the morning
Look out the window
And see my garden covered with frost.
Jack Frost has been last night
And covered the grass with speckles of dust.
I wake up in the morning,
The sun shines through the window
And tells me that I need to get up
And go outside to play.
I wake up in the morning,
Go outside and I step on something
That crushes under my feet.
I look to see what it is
And it's the colourful leaf
That has fallen and been carried by the wind,
I like to call this the seasons.

Lia Davies (13)
Whitchurch High School, Cardiff

The Eiffel Tower

The Eiffel Tower is an angel,
Watching where you walk
And every move you make.
She looks over Paris and watches every person.
In the night she lights up with happiness looking lovely,
And at any time you can see her
And she will be there for you shining with love!

Hannah Joyce (12)
Whitchurch High School, Cardiff

Green

The colour of green smells of fresh air
From the beautiful trees and grass
Where you see people play on grass
And all different things.
You see people climbing trees,
Having fun and laughter.

Mountains are covered in green
And beautiful country views of colour green
Where you see animals eating the fresh grass.

Trees give you fresh air for lungs
When you have nice beautiful walks
In the morning.

So you shouldn't forget all the things
That I've just told you.

Christopher Dench (11)
Whitchurch High School, Cardiff

Blue

Blue is the colour of the sparkling sea.
Blue is the colour of the clear sky.
Blue is the feeling of jumping in a swimming pool.
Blue is the sound of running water.
Blue is the taste of cold water.
Blue is the sound of the crashing waves.
Blue is the colour of the fish.
Blue is the feeling of a cold wet day.
Blue is the smell of the splashing raindrops.
Blue is the taste of a cold block of ice.
Blue is the sound of a flowing river.

James Tipping (12)
Whitchurch High School, Cardiff

Blue

Blue is the colour of coldness
Drifting through the air.
The waves are crashing on the shore,
Soggy, wet hair.

Blue is the colour of sadness
When people are feeling down.
Tears rolling past their cheeks,
The happiness has gone.

Blue is the colour of happiness
When newborn babies arrive,
People are crying with joy,
At the new baby boy.

So when you go out in the morning
And you see the colour blue,
Don't just think of sadness,
Think of joy and happiness too.

Madlen Cartwright (12)
Whitchurch High School, Cardiff

Train

I step on the train
With an edging pane.
It's my first time alone,
It's like a dog without a bone.
My stomach is ticking like a grandfather clock,
I haven't eaten all day by the way.
All these people looking at me,
It's like I'm on stage not earning a wage.
I wish I wasn't here,
I feel a little queer.

Jake Dunn (13)
Whitchurch High School, Cardiff

Christmas

C hildren all excited and jolly,
H appiness all over the world,
R udolph landing on my roof,
I t is the most wonderful time of the year,
S anta putting presents under our trees,
T rees decorated with lights, tinsel and baubles,
M ince pies left with milk for Santa,
A ll the children asleep waiting for the morning,
S now falling as everyone opens their presents.

Dan O'Connor (13)
Whitchurch High School, Cardiff

Football

F eet getting squashed,
O ranges at half-time,
O h scorching goal!
T rembling as the whistle blows,
B ad refereeing cost us the game,
A ngry managers at the touch line,
L atest score on the telly,
L ooking back at our performance.

Lloyd Davies (12)
Whitchurch High School, Cardiff

Apples

A sweet on the tongue
P articularly good for one's health
P acked full of vitamins and fructose
L arge, small or medium in size
E verlasting taste of autumn
S urprisingly satisfying when eaten.

Rebecca Thomas (12)
Whitchurch High School, Cardiff

Friends And Mates

F riends are girls who
R emember everything about you,
I magine a life without friends, my life would
E nd, as they are there for you every day
N ever-ending kindness
D edicated to making you happy
S uper special friends

A nyone needs someone as a friend or a mate
N ever being unhappy when they're around
D efinitely worth having

M ates are boys who
A nnoy you most times but
T hrough good times and bad will make you laugh
E very day they make me smile
S uper special mates!

Emily Irving (11)
Whitchurch High School, Cardiff

Christmas

C hristmas is a time of day when you have fun,
H aving presents put under your tree,
R ed ribbons on top of the wrapping paper,
I n the wrapping paper is something for you,
S omething special for you.
T ime when your family comes,
M um, Dad and everyone else
A nd then it's time to open your present,
S o you tear them up and get the toy.

Liam Creed (11)
Whitchurch High School, Cardiff

Colour

Yellow!
The sun gleaming on a summer day,
Breaking through spring,
Forever wanting to shine.

Yellow!
A juicy banana,
Waiting in a lunch box,
Waiting for a mouth.

Green!
A tree growing in the sun,
Its leaves shining like emeralds,
Hoping not to be cut into darkness.

Green!
Meadows of thick luscious grass,
Cows flicking up their tails,
Ever chewing on and on.

Owen Lindsey (12)
Whitchurch High School, Cardiff

Spirit Of The Horse

I am as calm as the sea,
But as wild as lightning,
For I am the spirit of the horse.
The curve of my neck,
Lit by the fire in my heart
And the light in my eye.
I whisper to the thunder
I am the spirit of the horse.
As swift in my flight as an eagle
That ever soared into the clouds,
For I am the spirit of the horse!

Eleri Cadogan (14)
Whitchurch High School, Cardiff

Colours Of The Rainbow

Red

Red is the colour of romance,
Also the angry tiger's eye.

Orange

Orange is the colour of autumn with the leaves
Blowing in the monstrous winds.

Yellow

Yellow is the colour of the sun
With its bright rays giving us the power to see.

Green

Green is the colour of jealousy,
Sucking up the Earth's possessions.

Blue

Blue is the colour of coldness within people's
Hearts grabbing their attention.

Indigo

Indigo is the colour of calm tranquillity
Floating in cool bliss.

Violet

Violet is the colour of the flowers in spring,
Filling everyone's hearts with joy and care.

Samantha Bryant (11)
Whitchurch High School, Cardiff

The Personality Of A Person

As in many things, we start at the top with the brain,
the brain is our cleverest of parts,
he teaches us day by day.
If our personality was like him, we would be perfect in every way.
He is our intelligence and speaks for us most of the time.
The heart is our romance.
She is not as clever as the brain,
yet she is just as powerful, as she too can speak for us.
She makes us cry, laugh and show our emotion.
The arms and hands are like a husband and wife.
They work together, they are artistic.
For the hands to paint, they need the arms to support them.
For the arms to reach, they need the hands to grab.
As we come to the bottom, we reach the legs and arms,
they are our athletic persons.
It is them which make us run, jump and hop.
They are not just our athletic person, but our greatest friend,
as they support us, and we are always there.

Rachel Hanson (13)
Whitchurch High School, Cardiff

The Fiery Furnaces, Green Grass And The Sky

I see the colour red,
It makes me feel like I'm on a beach
Feeling the sun burning on me like a beam of light.

The grass is so green
That it looks like it's far, far away
But will still grow anyway.

The sky is so strong
That you can see it from a mile away,
Blowing in the breeze
Like an elephant blowing his horn.

Charity Muchunga (11)
Whitchurch High School, Cardiff

Elvo

Everyone has me at one time in their life
but I cannot be bought or sold.

I can make you happy for years
and I can make you miserable at times.

Sometimes you think I'm wonderful
at others you hate me.

You know when I'm there
yet you cannot see me or feel me.

Some people think they can't live without me
whereas others think they don't need me.

I can come between people
but I can bring others closer.

I can make you have butterflies in your stomach
I can make your life a dream
I can turn your world upside down
but I am the greatest gift in the world.

What am I?
What am I to you?
Am I lovely or am I disgusting?
Do you want me?

Ellis Morgan (12)
Whitchurch High School, Cardiff

The Colour Blue

Blue is the colour of the deep blue sea,
Blue is the colour that makes me feel cold,
Blue is the colour of Powerade (my fave drink),
Blue is the colour of my face when I am ill,
Blue is the colour of the clear sky,
Blue is the feeling when a drink slips into my mouth,
Blue is my favourite colour!

Shona Fraser-Skuse (11)
Whitchurch High School, Cardiff

The Poet

He sits,
Pen in hand,
There was more paper in the bin,
Than in a forest,
The pen is now in his mouth,
His eyes are scrunched,
He wracks his brain,
His pen is so unused it has cobwebs on the nib,
His eyes widen,
He sits up straight,
His pen is now moving at the speed of light,
There is a long pause,
He stops writing,
The poem is good and doesn't he know it,
He finishes it off with the title,
'The Poet'.

Ryan Looker (12)
Whitchurch High School, Cardiff

The Man And His Shoe

The man and his shoe
Went to the loo.
They thought it was mean,
They thought it was clean,
But they never found out it was a washing machine!
They skipped back home,
Behind the dome,
Into their little shoe box,
It was warm,
It was cosy
Except for the neighbour who was very, very nosy.

Jac Jones (12)
Whitchurch High School, Cardiff

My Lies

I can tell you a few lies
That my nan calls 'porky pies'
You can tell in my eyes
That I'm telling lies

I can tell a few lies
And sometimes my brother cries
When I tell a load of lies
That he ate all the pies

I can tell a few lies
And my mum really sighs
When I tell a bunch of lies
That I put a few flies
In the Hallowe'en pies

I can tell a few lies
And my dad asks why
I made my brother cry
And all I do is make a lie.

Sam Perkins (11)
Whitchurch High School, Cardiff

Christmas!

On Christmas Eve
Everything is quiet,
Though minds are full of cheer,
In every thought
They race through lists,
Of gifts that are very near.

It's Christmas Day!
Snow's all around,
Now crowds rush down the stairs,
Paper flies,
Eyes open wide
To the surprise that lies inside.

Hannah Colman (13)
Whitchurch High School, Cardiff

The Four Seasons

When spring arrives
With birds in flight,
Daffodils and tulips grow,
We have seen the last
Of the winter snow.

Summer follows with day so bright,
Lighter evenings, shorter nights.
Our days are spent
Lying in the sun,
With lots of jobs
That have to be done.

Suddenly the leaves are brown,
The wind in the trees
Has a very strong quiver.
We then find ourselves
With quite a shiver.

Autumn is here,
Out come the coats.
Winter is coming,
It won't be long.

Then Christmas gives us all a boost
And the little red robin comes out to roost.
Festive church bells clearly ring
Which tells us the season will soon be spring.

Caitlin Davies (13)
Whitchurch High School, Cardiff

Football

Football is a crazy game
Players run and jump
And go insane.

The whistle goes
The crowd goes wild
I watch my dad act
Like a child.

I never thought this
Could be fun
But so much better
When Man U won.

As we hear
The other supporters moan
We smile and start our
Long walk home.

Danielle Yardley (12)
Whitchurch High School, Cardiff

What Am I?

It's where beautiful creatures live
But not on the land
What am I?
When the moon shines down on it
It sparkles in the light
I'm blue, sometimes clear
But I'm not the sky
What am I?
I surround islands and countries
But I'm not the air
What am I?
I am the sea.

Claire James (12)
Whitchurch High School, Cardiff

Football

As we wait nervously to run on,
The crowd shouts our names.
The butterflies begin to kick in,
It is time.

A horrible clunking and scraping noise is made,
As our footwear hits the ground as we stream out.
We hit the light, the stadium erupts,
We line up.

The whistle sounds, no more nerves,
The ball is lofted through the air
And it scuttles quickly across the turf.
The noise is unbearable,
The crowd is going wild.
Into the box the ball is chipped,
A gigantic leap,
The ball is accurately placed on his head,
Goal!

Josh Carbis (13)
Whitchurch High School, Cardiff

Wales - Simply The Best

The green, green grass of home is here,
The sheep go 'bore-baa',
There are several great footie teams,
Wales is the best by far!

The Manics rock the city,
The Millennium Stadium yells,
The Stereophonics live here,
Wales is completely swell!

Saint David is the patron saint,
To make it can't have been wrong,
Cardiff is the capital city,
Wales is the bomb!

David Heslop (11)
Whitchurch High School, Cardiff

The Mine

Inside the lethal mine lies an even deadlier creature,
It seals itself inside a torturous tomb in which no good is found,
You cannot smell it,
Or hear it,
And not even see it,
This foul beast is . . . *gas!*

Its eyes are like cats spying on everything and everyone,
Silent, suspicious and terrifying,
As innocent miners hack away at the dark, dank walls
It watches with excitement,
Nearer and nearer they chop, unaware of the danger
That lurks in amongst the shadows.

Finally a chink is decimated by a rusty pick axe,
The gas grins with anticipation and excitement that soon
He will be free from his icy tomb,
At last the poor miner strikes it,
Eagerly the gas rushes out to cause terror,
A few seconds later, *bang!*
The miners are never to be seen again.

Jonathan Williams (11)
Whitchurch High School, Cardiff

Hallowe'en

On the 30th of October,
When the moon is bright,
Witches and ghouls come out at night,

Black cats will creep around,
Spying on children without a sound,
Owls will hide in trees at night,
Turning their heads, their eyes filled with spite.

Dress up, have fun, go out
Beware, don't scream or shout!

Carys Trace (11)
Whitchurch High School, Cardiff

Colours Here And There

Red is the colour of danger, here, there and everywhere,
It's the colour of a warrior fighting on a battlefield.

Yellow is the colour of burning fire flickering all of the night,
It's the colour of the gigantic sun looking down on us.

Green is the colour of grass and trees swaying in the breeze,
It's the colour of mountains long away in the distance.

Blue is the colour of the sky going on and on,
It's the colour of ice in the waiting still lake.

White is the colour of snow falling down on you and me,
It's the colour of clouds all in shapes and sizes.

Black is the colour of darkness all alone in an empty room,
It's the colour of worried faces. It's the colour of sadness.

Johanna Lewis (12)
Whitchurch High School, Cardiff

Icy Blue

This colour is a smooth, soft colour that helps me relax
And calm down.
This colour is also the colour that sends tingles
And shivers down my spine.
Icy-blue the colour I find as a cold colour that is trapped
In a block of ice.
Icy-blue the colour of the Antarctica sky with the crisp
White snow lying untouched under the sky.
Some people see the colour as a warm colour
But I see it as a cold colour trapped in a block of ice.

Bethan Webber (11)
Whitchurch High School, Cardiff

The Mountain

I look straight ahead,
And what do I see?
A beautiful sight
Towering over me,
Breaking through the clouds like a skyscraper
Dotted with trees,
Some are laden with fruit,
Others a spectacle of colour.
A fresh stream,
Glistening in the midday sun,
Winds it way down and off,
Further than the eye can see.
As I make my way up I notice the ferns that cover it,
As snow does a field.
But in no time at all the climb is over,
I have reached the top.
There in the middle is a stone pillar,
It stands at the very top,
The end of a brilliant walk and the glorious sense of achievement.
Quickly I clamber up and look upon the sight below me.
Though what a wondrous one it is!
The street lamps glistening and lighting up the roads,
The green forests streaming over the lush fields.
It almost puts this to shame!
As I skid down,
I take a last look at the fleeing sheep that make themselves scarce.
One last look at the tumbling rocks
And one last look at the view below me.
But nothing,
Nothing!
Is so beautiful as the mountain!

Charlotte Williams (11)
Whitchurch High School, Cardiff

Christmas

C hristmas is a time for joy
H owever to kids a time for presents
wR apped up all with a bow on top
I mmaculate presents, big and tall
S anta Claus coming to deliver presents
T ime to send those letters
M assive presents
A ll what you want
S o get ready kids, Santa Claus is coming.

Yanni Haralambos (12)
Whitchurch High School, Cardiff

Dolphins

D olphins are cute and play all day,
O ver the waves they jump,
L augh and have fun with them,
P lough the sea like them,
H old on tight for the ride of your life,
I want to swim with dolphins one day,
N ow when I see them,
S miling with their skin like shiny rubber!

Zoe Grima (12)
Whitchurch High School, Cardiff

Christmas Has Begun

Christmas has begun,
The wonderful world of white,
Lots of sparkly flakes and lots of good fun.
Angels reach from Heaven and leave about seven.
Pure, fresh and white snow falling from the sky,
As people go into their stores with lots of gifts to buy.

Shakah Meah (11)
Whitchurch High School, Cardiff

Red (Colour)

Red.
Red is the taste of a squished tomato.
Red is the feeling in you when you are proud.
Red is the smile of red-rose lips.
Red is the colour of a sour punch.
Red is the sound of a rampaging bull.
Red is the smell of a Valentine's rose.
Red is the colour of death blood.
Red is the sign of love.
Red is the smell of ashes of a fire.
Red is the feeling of pepperoni after a hot pizza.
Red is the heart that keeps you alive.
Red is the colour of the liver that wriggles inside you.
Red is the date of late autumn.
Red is the sign for danger.

Megan Hession (11)
Whitchurch High School, Cardiff

Red

As the volcano erupts, the suffocating ash blots out the sky -
The red is coming.

The siren screeches as the flames grow, the city dies -
The red is coming.

The tiger roars as his jungle is crushed -
The red is coming.

All love is stopped by the demon's cry -
The red is coming.

The world falls prey to the angry force -
The red has arrived.

You hear the screech, the roar, the cry, your whole life crumbles away -
The red has arrived, and it has come for *you*.

Thomas Pacey (11)
Whitchurch High School, Cardiff

The Colours Of The Sun

Red is the bloody colour of the sun,
it reminds me how people shout and run,
from the evil that lies within the sun,
it's like the Devil who is having so much fun,
killing people who live in the sun.

Yellow is the light colour of the sun,
it reminds me how people of God stopped the Devil
                                and made him run,
using their powers of the sun,
saving people, maybe a tonne,
so the people are safe in the sun.

Orange is the two colours mixed together in the sun,
it's like the people who run,
from the battle of good and evil in the sun,
they don't know who to cheer for because they're none.

So these are the colours of the sun,
it's up to you to choose good, evil or none.

Nader Khundakji (11)
Whitchurch High School, Cardiff

Blue

Blue is the colour of a fresh sky,
Blue is the look of me when I come off the bumpy ferry trip,
Blue is the taste of pure dazzling water,
Blue is the feel of Christmas, the icicles hanging off the gutter,
Blue is the colour of a newborn baby's smile,
Blue is the colour of a bluebell that is blooming in every way,
Blue is the feeling of being happy on a bright summer's day,
Blue is the taste of ice cream as it quenches my hunger,
Blue is the sound of the wind as it rushes past my face,
Blue is the smell of dolphins gliding through the Atlantic.

Hope Rees (11)
Whitchurch High School, Cardiff

Blue Rush

    A wall of blue
        crashes above me
           growing
              climbing
                  towering
    until it curls
    with the grey reef all
    round me, the sound
    of the water gushing down
    that blue wall with
    the smell of my tropical wax
       as
         I
           wait
           for
                my
                  big
                      Wednesday
                      to
                  come
  the wall is roaring in
    my ears, carving down
      the face then I turn
        off
           the
                blue rush
                      I
                        can't
                          wait
                          for
                        tomorrow,
                        to
                        go surfing.

Alex Wilson (12)
Whitchurch High School, Cardiff

Space

A comet, slashing, slicing through the atmosphere,
blazing black as it smoulders into atoms,
supanovas; gunpowder clinging to every star until old age,
then eruptions, rumbling throughout the galaxy,
the black hole, soul sucker and life absorber,
forcefully wrenching, destroying the Milky Way.
The moon; a ghastly substance of tranquillity, the Earth's shield.
Stars; observant orbs scattered like poppy fields
across the jewelled sky.
Jupiter; the space, spy, seeking the life form it so desperately wants.
Our solar system; a vast wheel, rotating around a fiery axle,
motoring through space.
Rockets; fiery arrows penetrating our atmosphere
on voyages to distant moons.

This is man's dream come true!

Oliver Jackson (11)
Whitchurch High School, Cardiff

My Best Friend

It was in the bright, sunny school field
where lots of people were shouting and screaming.
She was running around like a zooming sports car,
her smooth, silky hair blowing in the cool breeze.
She was wearing a short, denim skirt
with a pale, minty-green top.
Her big, cheesy grin was dazzling,
her sparkly green eyes glistened.
She said to me, 'Come on, let's have fun!'
Her highlighted hair shone against the bright blue sky,
a big, shiny rainbow in the distance.
She grabbed my hand, then spun me around
and that was the end of that!

Rachel Nealon (12)
Whitchurch High School, Cardiff

White

As the day starts snow starts to fall
snowflakes floating in the air

Jack Frost is coming down the hill with his friends, the yetis
wrapped in scarves and gloves.

As the sun rises, weddings begin
as God watches the yetis begin.

As they get closer they start to melt
into a piece of felt.

Charlie Winch (11)
Whitchurch High School, Cardiff

Life

Green, crisp leaves flowing
down from lofty trees above.

The ancient, tall, tangled trees are being destroyed
by the red, flaming fires of industry.

Burning like the sun,
those fire-breathing demons, destroyers of all,
like the Devil in Hell.

Vincent Godfrey (11)
Whitchurch High School, Cardiff

What Can You See?

When you look out the window you can see,
Lots of people looking at me,

Look to the left, you can see,
A big portrait of the sea,
Look to the right and you can see,
A few birds looking to sea.

What do you see when you see me?

Stephanie Ellis (11)
Whitchurch High School, Cardiff

Red

Dicing with death,
Fiery breath.
Cunning and sly,
Tiger's fierce cry.
Confident, bold,
Bossy, controlled.
Dangerous fight
Burning red light!

Restless volcano erupts with a flash,
Brave matador, darting, waving his sash.
Scaly dragon breathing fire,
Embarrassed blushing of a liar.
Devil's grave sneer,
Stabbing with fear.
Explosion, carnage, slash of a knife,
Pools of blood - fluid of life.
Sunset so beautiful, end of a day,
May courage be the dominant ray.

Kate Bowley (11)
Whitchurch High School, Cardiff

Autumn Leaves

Autumn leaves are falling
Red, yellow and brown
Falling softly on the ground
They make no sound.
They fall on your head,
They fall on your feet,
They fall on the pavement,
They fall in the street.
They fall everywhere . . .

Sarah Jones (11)
Whitchurch High School, Cardiff

My Family!

My fabulous mum,
She's number one,
She's certainly not dumb,
I think I've won!

My great dad,
He's footy mad,
His cooking's yum,
It rests in my tum!

My annoying sister,
Is my skin and blister,
Who can be alright,
When you see her in daylight!
But you better watch out if she's about in the night!
That's my excellent family!

Jessica Davies (11)
Whitchurch High School, Cardiff

That's White For Me

Fluffy clouds floating
Wedding bells ringing
Little sheep flying
That's white for me!

Soft lights shining
Chilly snow falling
Angels float from Heaven
That's white for me!

Skiing down snow slopes
Bubbles daydreaming on the moon
Doves drifting on ice
That's white for me!

Poppy Shillabeer (11)
Whitchurch High School, Cardiff

My Friends

My friend is called Jess,
And she's the best,
She's so cool,
She will always be my friend,
Until the end.

And then there's Caitlin,
She's so smart,
She's really reliable,
And always there,
She will always be my friend,
Until the end.

And I'm called Becks,
I'm very funny,
I'm always up for a laugh,
I can be quite daft,
But I'll always be there,
For my friends.

Rebecca Leonard (11)
Whitchurch High School, Cardiff

My Colour Poem

Drifting flakes drift down from the heavens,
God has blessed each one,
The wedding is coming,
Bride and groom together at last.
Dear Mother is ill,
She lies still,
Pale and unwell in her bed,
She is dreaming, slowly,
Drifting away.

Sarah Gould (11)
Whitchurch High School, Cardiff

A White Winter

White waves crash on the shore,
In the freezing cold breeze,
The snowflakes fall from the sky with grace.
The flakes are as cold as ice cream.
People walk across the beach,
Holding each other to keep warm.
Even with their scarves and gloves on.
All families huddle together.

Dionne Morgans (11)
Whitchurch High School, Cardiff

Colour Poem

Peace from above comes sparkling down,
As the moonlight is still and dead.
Frosty mountains give me the winter chills
As clouds drift down and the clouds freeze.

Pale angels float down to save,
They bring us peace on this fresh day,
Yetis rise from the dead and still,
At the top of the mountain they're cold and ill.

Luke Robson (11)
Whitchurch High School, Cardiff

The Fiery Dragon

A dragon lays in its lair,
Breathing fire all day long,
It defends its only home,
It's ruthless to anyone who dares to come,
The yellow eyes are enough to scare you,
Above its lair is a sign that reads *Danger*,
The dragon's heart is only small,
It doesn't really love anything at all.

Jordan Sugarman (11)
Whitchurch High School, Cardiff

Seasons

Winter is a time of joy,
To play around with Christmas toys,
Throw snowballs at each other,
Pulling crackers with your brother,
Skating around with girls and boys.

Spring is a time of peace and new birth,
Daffodils shooting up from the earth,
Baby chicks coming out of their eggs,
Flowers brushing around your legs,
Spring is a time of great mirth.

Summer is a time of very hot sun,
When lots of children have loads of fun,
Building sandcastles on the beach,
Crushing them with a single reach,
Summer is here so the sun has come.

Autumn is a time of leafless trees,
Wherever you walk you're walking on leaves,
Beautiful colours all across the land,
No one could describe it as bland,
Now autumn has been there are no more bees.

Gareth Lewis (13)
Whitchurch High School, Cardiff

Heaven

As the angels glide in God's Heaven, doves perch peacefully,
As the sparkling icy flakes of the winter season fall,
They fall like bubbles through the cold, winter air,
As they float down to the frosty layers of twinkling snow.
Small figures down below are wrapped up in scarves and gloves.
As the clouds disappear a yellow light fills up the sea-blue sky.
Spring has come and colourful flowers blossom,
Pinks, reds, purples, whites,
The view from Heaven is a wonderful sight.

Paige Wickers (12)
Whitchurch High School, Cardiff

Important People

A small tortoiseshell cat,
Inside a cardboard box,
Inside a cosy, large house,
This very small cat trying hard to destroy this small box,
Then suddenly she stops!
Then goes whizzing around the house skidding on the wooden floor,
Her coffee-brown legs scamper quickly across the floor
As fast as they can carry her.
After a moment of madness this scatty cat turns into a tranquil purr
And jumps up onto my kind mum's lap and falls asleep.
This tortoiseshell cat jumps around like a jolly flea.
This contradicting cat, shy and inquisitive
Could change at any moment.
The colours that I would put with this mini lioness
Are pink and red because sometimes she is really mad
And sometimes she is really sweet.
If I could turn this cat into an animal that roams freely in the jungle,
I would call this cat a lioness because her colours match
And her inquisitive ways remind everyone of this fast and free animal.

Sophie Baker (11)
Whitchurch High School, Cardiff

The London Guard

The Tower of London is not just a tower it's an old tired guard
who has been standing, watching London for hundreds of years.
Taking care of all those crime-seeking citizens
of different times in history.
Hundreds of prisoners have been and gone,
birds nested, tourists have visited, and still the old man stands there,
higher than anything around.
Guarding the precious crown jewels and priceless artifacts.
No doubt longing to sit down but not being able to because
it would damage everything he spent all those years protecting.
And standing, guarding London
is how he shall spend the rest of his life!

Elizabeth Shipston (12)
Whitchurch High School, Cardiff

White

Drifting flakes fall,
People ski down the mountains,
Wrapped in scarves and gloves.

Crunching through the cold, chilling snow,
Harsh Jack Frost is on his way,
People fill with happiness,
As the snowflakes fall.

Fluffy white clouds,
Fill with the last snow,
As winter goes.

The snow is over,
The chill has gone,
Gloves and hats go away,
As ice creams are on their way.

Saskia Lehane (11)
Whitchurch High School, Cardiff

Red

Flickering flames, smoking in the air,
roaring like a tiger, fierce with anger,
the volcano erupts, lava spills,
like dragon's breath, angry and evil.

Lava trickling down, down and down,
too hot to freeze,
like boiling water, sweaty and bubbly,
turning into ash.

Fire screams in my face,
run away, never ever stop!
Finally I have come to an end,
of this dangerous place, that I wouldn't recommend!

Catherine Williams (11)
Whitchurch High School, Cardiff

Black

The colour of dark,
Not a glimmer of light,
Then a figure appears . . .
The angel of night.

Waiting, waiting,
For a dream to catch,
To change to a nightmare,
There's no escape.

Complete silence as twelve strikes,
No sound can be heard,
Nothing can be seen,
As a young child's dream,
Becomes a dream to forget.

Then a shimmer of light,
Scares the night away,
As the angel screams,
She fades away.

Black,
The colour of night.

Alex Newton (12)
Whitchurch High School, Cardiff

White

Drifting flakes fall,
Angels from Heaven,
Peace spread by our holy Lord.
The moon glistening with the stars, singing in one song.

Jack Frost arrives with winter chills,
Scarves and gloves wrapped tight,
Mother, dear Mother, pale as a ghost,
With a cold, and tears trickling down her face.

Bronwyn Northcott (11)
Whitchurch High School, Cardiff

A Dream

A fluttering dream in the eyes,
a wedding,
snow is falling,
God overlooks from Heaven
above the drifting clouds
like sheep walking in the sunshine.
A harsh breeze
blows from the north,
soon to cover the world in white.
It comes closer and closer
but joy was followed,
a dark air filled the sky,
it spread
like an illness
and every time it
came close
there was death.
A dark wind blew
in all directions,
2 minutes after
there was nothing left,
when God saw this
He threw His power
to Earth
and every life
was restored.

Jamie Kingsford (11)
Whitchurch High School, Cardiff

Bobby

B obby the dog is my dog!
O f course I love him to bits, why wouldn't you?
B ecause he is so cute, he is a small Yorkshire terrier,
B obby likes his cuddles in the morning, to get attention,
Y et most importantly he is my little bundle of joy!

Gabrielle Regan (11)
Whitchurch High School, Cardiff

Red Battle

Red means vile
Just like death upon the Nile
Red like Hell
All love has faded
Evil has invaded
The dark armies then will come
When the sun is 1000001
The apocolypse is coming
You can hear the evil drumming
They will come like galloping cavalry
They will draw swords and fight
You'll get more than a fright
We will fight upon this night
We are as angry as wild boars
The battle will begin
For hope and love
We must win.

Michael Ley (11)
Whitchurch High School, Cardiff

My Auntie's Two Dogs

Their faces are small and cute,
They run like a barking hoot,
They're really fluffy and white,
They remind me of a bright kite,
Their ears stick up,
They are two cute pups.

They're very cute to cuddle,
And like running in puddles,
Their tails are short and spiky,
They're just so mighty.

That's Ros and Scott.

Hannah Lewis (11)
Whitchurch High School, Cardiff

About My Mum

My mum and me would go to the beach
the warm sand below my feet
and the seaweed would tickle me.
The crabs would run like black and white cheetahs.
It was a wonderful day.
The fish would be swishing and swaying
side to side, glowing like two rockets
in the big blue sky.

My mum sits down
on the big, strong but soft chair
with the dark and milky-white chocolate.
Bit by bit she would crunch it
the chocolate would melt on her tongue.
The way my mum talks is like an angel
drifting into the air with a harp
it would sound soft and beautiful.

My mum's hair is long
and blonde like Rapunzel
it's soft as silk and hard and beautiful like gold
if my mum was a colour she would be yellow like the sun
blue is cold and red-warm inside to look after me.

Jack Haberfield (11)
Whitchurch High School, Cardiff

White Winter Mornings

White winter morning,
Whispers awake the snoring child,
Mutters of the wind wipes the breeze away from the window.

Ice grips the trees,
Holding them prisoner,
Snow starts to fall,
Silently and softly.

Jordan Gibbs (11)
Whitchurch High School, Cardiff

Winter Christmas

The little boy shivers
In the cold wind's grasp
A plague of frost fills the village
A clear shimmer of crystal in the sky
Frozen snowmen standing like a motionless army
Crunchy grass crumbling in the shape of footsteps
Blinding lights on an exciting tree
A slight jingle in the distant sky
Families gliding on thick ice
Children throwing icy snowballs
Parents cooking in the packed kitchen
A shocking 'Yes!' from the next room
A little girl opens a present
A blue-eyed, blonde-haired doll lay in her hands
A delightful aroma came from the kitchen
A great day, Christmas Day.

Alex Amor (11)
Whitchurch High School, Cardiff

Who Is The Millennium Stadium?

He is front page news,
But not cheap, Cardiff's local celebrity,
His fans follow him in awe,
When they come pouring through his open door.

He looks like an inverted spider,
His strong sturdy legs,
Soaring up into the sky,
And viewed from above is Cardiff's blinking green eye.

He is someone you can always find,
His floodlight's a guiding light, a beacon to all who visit his city,
He is around all through the day,
He is never lost or far away.

Vashti Williamson (12)
Whitchurch High School, Cardiff

Me And My Dad

At the Millennium Stadium with my dad
The stadium's packed to see the Welsh play
I can't see because of people bigger than me
My dad gives me a boost so I can see.

My dad is chanting
Goal! Goal!
And I start laughing!
And he does as well.

My dad is in his Wales top
And I am as well
He has dragons on his face, flags in his hand
But lots of people love footie as much as my dad.

My dad is the colour yellow
Happy and joyful
Especially when he goes to a Wales game
But sometimes he's like the colour red.

In all the streets and pubs
Shouting and chanting
1-0 to the champions
While the opposition moan and groan.

Scott Saunders (12)
Whitchurch High School, Cardiff

Hallowe'en

H is for holidays
A is for all the sweets
L is for late nights out
L is for lollies everywhere
O is for October, since it's in October
W is for all the weird costumes
E is for eggs all over the place
E is for all the evening parties
N is for the naughty boy who throws the eggs!

Ashley Said (11)
Whitchurch High School, Cardiff

My Dad

I can see a beautiful beach,
With warm, golden sands,
And a tropical, glistening ocean.
There is no one on the sand,
Except for me.

> I am looking out to the horizon
> Where I can just about see
> The silhouette of my dad
> Leaning out of his sailing boat.

My dad is wearing a T-shirt
And swimming trunks.
He's tall with brown hair,
Blowing in the breeze,
As he zooms through the water
In his sailing boat.

> My dad would be blue,
> He is caring, mostly calm and
> Likes to have fun.
> He has a good sense of humour.

It is almost as if I am
Looking through a window
Showing a perfect world,
But, outside,
Things are not perfect.

Bryony James (11)
Whitchurch High School, Cardiff

Wales

W ales, the land of my fathers
A land of hope and glory
L and of hills and beautiful scenes
E verlasting is our spirit
S un, we have not, but it doesn't dampen our morale.

Alun Welsh (12)
Whitchurch High School, Cardiff

My Mum

Mum on the long beach in a green chair
Surrounded by shining sand and big blue waves
Children playing and making sandcastles
Babies in armbands enjoying themselves

Mum is eating a mint and vanilla ice cream with a dark Flake
It is melting slowly
After, playing bat and ball in the deep sea
Also the shiny waves splash
Making her fall over

Mum wearing her black swimming costume
With her colourful hat and cool sunglasses
Also putting on suncream
The sun is roaring hot on her arms and legs

My mum would be yellow
That makes her feel jolly and happy
It makes her fall asleep
The gleaming sun so hot and a warming smile

People out in a restaurant close by
Eat with a little whisper
Quiet music is played by violins, keyboards and other instruments
Also people dance, enjoying themselves.

Bethan Johnston (11)
Whitchurch High School, Cardiff

I Wish . . .

I wish I was on a tropical island lying on the beach!
I wish I could have chocolate, chocolate, chocolate!
I wish I was a fairy with sparkly silver wings!
I wish I could swim in tropical blue waters!
I wish I had a robot who could do everything for me!
I wish the world could all be friends and peaceful!
I wish . . . I wish . . . I wish . . . for a lot of things!

Aimee Harrison (11)
Whitchurch High School, Cardiff

My Mum

There is a snug little room,
With a bright glowing fire,
There sits my mother,
Reading a book of love,
Toes curling with delight,
Turning the page on a roll.

She places the book down,
But soon goes back,
Her bright hazel-brown eyes shine in the light,
Her hair shining a dark brown,
Her smile making me feel relaxed and happy,
She is smiling and looking cheerful.

If I was to say she was a colour
I would say she was an orange colour
Because she is always happy,
And sometimes she can be extra happy.

If you look outside,
You would see children in the snow,
They would be building a snowman,
And having fun.

Sophie Nash (11)
Whitchurch High School, Cardiff

Model Of Paris

The Eiffel Tower is a supermodel,
brightly striding down the catwalk of Paris!
Its admirers taking pictures for newspapers and magazines!
Its shiny, golden gown swaying sideways after every step!
Its diamonds, rubies and sparkling sapphires and lights that flicker
non-stop through the dark night!
People pushing and pulling to get on the lift
just to talk face to face with glamourous models!
That's what the Eiffel Tower really is!

Charlotte Chappell (13)
Whitchurch High School, Cardiff

Important People - My Mum

My mum watching telly
Sitting on the black leather suite
With the cream walls around her
As she eats her cherry cream chocs

My dog laying on the rug in front of the fire
Me laying down on the sofa
Watching 'EastEnders' and 'Corrie' with my mum

She had her nightclothes and dressing gown on
With her hightlighted hair

She's the colour of lilac
Pretty and perfumed
Happy and joyful
The best colour around

My mum
The best mum ever.

Stevie Morgan (12)
Whitchurch High School, Cardiff

CN Tower - Cruel, Nasty Tower

Towering over all the rest,
think it's better? It's the *best!*
With yellow bug-like arms of steel
looking so strange . . . it's surreal.
With all the other small buildings below,
with the tower's example they all try to follow.
With its long, slim body,
and a large head to look over all.
Leaning to see everyone,
make sure you don't fall!
Its giant rotating head sees all,
like a wise old owl.
Bullying all the shorter towers,
frankly it's just foul!

Samuel Paul Thomas
Whitchurch High School, Cardiff

My Mum

She is sitting in the lounge,
On the green and beige sofa.
The TV is on and she is very quiet.
It is dark with only candles as her light.

She is watching TV,
While sipping a cup of Coke,
The candles are melting a lot so she blows them out,
Then the lady leaves the room and goes upstairs.

That lady is my mum,
She is wearing a skirt with a flowery top,
She has brown hair and a big smile.
I see her bright blue eyes looking at me.

She is the colour pink,
Because it is a kind colour,
A caring colour,
And that's like my mum.

Outside, my dad has come home from work,
And my mum goes to see him,
Then she comes inside and goes back to her work,
She is a great mum.

Kate McCarthy (11)
Whitchurch High School, Cardiff

The Eiffel Tower

The Eiffel Tower is a French gendarme
watching over Paris.
Standing there, tall and proud,
as people gaze and stare.
Bright flashing lights shooting like a movie star,
very proudly, striking a pose for the paparazzi's cameras.
When all the people have gone in,
he's just a normal ornament to the French city.
It all starts again in the morning,
the normal routine of a day for this Parisian policeman.

Anna Batten (12)
Whitchurch High School, Cardiff

England Cricket Team

The great ground of Lord's
towers above the city
the excited crowd streams through the turnstiles
and the players start to have butterflies

England wait on the balcony
tapping their new spikes
Trescothick and Strauss pad up
and nervously pick up their bats

The openers walk out on the newly-cut grass
and a cheer goes up from the crowd
the batsmen practise their cricket shots
they must feel very proud

England are all in their whites
cheering from the balcony
the batsmen are off to a good start
let's hope they can carry on!

Those outside are getting restless
because they are missing the game
they can see the ball high above Lord's
and are listening to the crowd's applause

Why didn't they get there earlier?

Tom Salmon (11)
Whitchurch High School, Cardiff

Dolphins

Diving gracefully through white breakers
In an Ocean teeming with life
Dancing, Leaping through crystal waters
As children, Play through the foam
Bodies sleek and Honed as an athlete's
Twisting, turning like Impressive torpedoes
Calling from the depths of Nemo's world

Oh I wish I could swim like a *dolphin*.

Rachel Bodger (12)
Whitchurch High School, Cardiff

Poem Of London Eye

There it stands, tall and wide
Looking over the city, like a policeman
The capsules are the eyes, constantly circling the sky, keeping an eye
If you make trouble, the eyes will see and make trouble for thee

Not one would dream of getting past the strict, over watching guard
The Houses of Parliament, the bridge and the Thames lie safely
Within its watchful bounds
The policeman, keeping all that it surveys safe and sound

Protector of the city and all that's held within
When trouble knocks at its door, it will not let it in
The people feel much safer since the policeman's watchful guard
And all are keen to ensure that their city is not marred

So continue watching over and keeping safe the sights
Your ever-watchful guard keeps them safe both day and night
For this the people are grateful and thank you from their hearts
And in keeping London safe, they promise they too will play their part

As times go by
We live in peace
Under the gaze
Of the *London Eye*.

Daniel Draper (12)
Whitchurch High School, Cardiff

An Aztec Giant

Down, down the blood goes, staining steps like old ragged clothes.
Up, up the priest goes, dragging prisoners to and fro.
Tear, tear the knife goes, organs standing in columns and rows.
Splat, splat the heart goes, spitting blood like a wild cat.
Roll, roll the carcass goes, falling blindly like a muddy mole.
Such is the life of an Aztec temple, a sleeping giant in the
                              baking Mexican sun.

Timothy Vincent (12)
Whitchurch High School, Cardiff

Important People

In my blue bedroom,
Sat me and my best friend, Bethan
We sat on my bed,
Talked, joked and had such fun

>She's sitting on my bed,
>Talking and joking,
>Laughing so hard,
>Tears run down her face.

>>If she was a colour
>>She'd have to be yellow.
>>Happy, funny and cheerful
>>Always a smile is on her face.

We look outside,
More friends arrive,
Smiling joyfully,
They're coming in to join us.

Rhiannon Collins (11)
Whitchurch High School, Cardiff

It's Always There

Is as red as blood,
And as sour as raspberries,
Like a crashing flood,
As hatred ferries,
Burning away,
As on one point it is tied,
Words sharp as knives,
Stabbing through the air,
Breaking old ties,
As though they weren't there,
The smoky smell wafting through,
So thick and musky, nothing sweet can seep through,
Anger is there, always trying to break through,
The only thing allowing it to get through is you.

Emma Williams (13)
Whitchurch High School, Cardiff

The Statue Of Liberty

The Statue of Liberty stands tall and proud on the catwalk
                              that is New York.
People from everywhere around the world come and see her.
Her elegant green dress glimmers in the sunshine.
She is surrounded by tourists,
They are the paparazzi of the model world,
They are always with her,
Taking photos and protecting her from her loving fans.
Everyone is astounded by her beauty.
Her name is commonly spoken.
Everyone knows who she is.
She never moves from that same spot.
She stands for everything New York believes in.
Freedom.

Catherine Stephens (12)
Whitchurch High School, Cardiff

The Sydney Opera House

I imagine the Sydney Opera House as a Hollywood film star,
With the press photographers never too far,
He has the latest hairstyle,
And all the fashion experts as well as a glittering smile,
With all the wonderful voices,
That are played within,
Which create a din,
He has a humorous side,
Like a comedy act going on inside his head,
He represents Australia,
He flies the flag,
He lives by the harbour,
Watching the boats that pass,
A shining white light in a glamorous world.

Jamie Humphrys (12)
Whitchurch High School, Cardiff

The Statue Of Liberty

The Statue of Liberty is no ordinary statue,
She is a security guard . . .
As all the ships of tourists enter America,
The eyes of the statue gleam down on them,
As she is looking for anything suspicious, yet smiling a welcome smile,
At night when the country of America is sleeping,
The statue's torch lights up like a beacon,
So she can see if there is any danger heading towards America,
The statue also represents freedom,
Everyone in America is free,
They will not be harmed by any terrorists,
So when you enter America through the gateway of the
North Atlantic Ocean,
Beware as you are being watched,
By the Statue of Liberty!

Rebeca Evans (12)
Whitchurch High School, Cardiff

The Cops

These towers aren't towers, they're cops.
These cops are looking down on New York,
Standing high in the sky,
Seeing two men fighting.
They show them to the cell,
Then go back to the port.
They're looking out for crime,
And taking orders from their boss.
When these two big boys are in town,
No one messes around.
Remember these cops are looking at you!
They're looking at you like little ants,
They're making sure you're all right.
They are like a bulletproof jacket protecting the city.

Kyle Beal (12)
Whitchurch High School, Cardiff

The Arc De Triomphe

The Arc De Triomphe is not an arch,
She is a gymnast creating an arch shape with her body.
She is sturdy,
She is balanced,
Showing off her skills to all the people,
Looking around to see who is watching,
To see the people whose eyes she is catching.
She is pretty,
She is glamorous,
She wants the whole world to love her,
To stay there,
Just staring straight at her,
Never to leave her side.
However, at the end of the day,
This so-called glory disappears,
This so-called glory vanishes,
At the end of the day,
It's all gone.

Andrew Sleat (13)
Whitchurch High School, Cardiff

Eiffel Tower

The Eiffel Tower is the tour guide of Paris.
With his flicking lights,
Shining bright,
He draws everybody to him,
All through the night,
Being able to show where countries are,
With his beautiful arc,
And pointing arms,
Showing how far,
Calais - 10 miles,
Marseilles - 130 miles,
You can see the Eiffel Tower,
Wherever you are.

Scott Curtis (12)
Whitchurch High School, Cardiff

The Millennium Stadium

The Millennium Stadium is no stadium.
It's a screaming mouth. It makes lots of noise,
And it's full of girls and boys.
Even when the mouth is shut,
You can still hear the noise.
The mouth cries,
When Beckham skies,
The winning penalty,
And England lose the game.
The gems are the people,
As they leave the mouth,
Some happy, some sad.
This usually happens once a week,
But sometimes happens more.
Sometimes there are riots,
Where the mouth screams even more.
Sometimes there are boring games,
Where the mouth begins to snore.

William McMahon (12)
Whitchurch High School, Cardiff

Statue Of Liberty

The Statue of Liberty stands in peace,
She is very quiet, but all her other building friends make a riot,
She only screams when her Yankees win,
She fires the light of New York Stadium
And the hearts of American people.
No wonder New York is called 'the city that never sleeps',
Liberty always lights her torch,
She gets the fire from the sun,
Reaching high for the sky,
For some reason she finds it very fun,
An eternal symbol, a maternal symbol to a nation.

Tanvir Miah (12)
Whitchurch High School, Cardiff

The Mouth Of The Millennium Stadium

The Millennium Stadium roars passionately, supporting her
                                      team to the end,
The mouth of Cymru opens when all weather is good,
Ringing out with praise for the team when all is going well,
But when the weather turns bad she closes her gaping mouth,
She sings along to pop songs like a child with a personal CD,
And erupts into joy when Wales scores a goal,
But when Wales are losing she vomits angry people out as if ill,
The hisses ring rampant - ruling her great mouth,
But even when she rests her mouth and closes it tight,
The noise of the revs go out into the night,
Cars and motorbikes race round her mouth,
She inhales the exhaust and then breathes it out,
But she never removes those four white sticks and coughs out
                                        exploding colourful fire,
The greatness of her voice echoes eternally into the streets of Cardiff.

Patrick McDowell (12)
Whitchurch High School, Cardiff

Catwalk Queen

The Eiffel Tower is the new supermodel,
Strutting its stuff down the catwalk.
People standing and staring,
Arching their necks in amazement.
Cameras flashing at its brown dress
Shimmering bronze in the sunlight.
Her diamond accessories glow
Almost as if they're colourful lights
Lit up to make her stand out.
The Eiffel Tower is definitely
The most famous model of the catwalk!

Clarice Watkinson (12)
Whitchurch High School, Cardiff

Happiness

Happiness is like sunshine
Or sunflowers beneath a clear blue sky
Ladybirds clinging to flower stems
A light wind rustling the grass beneath our feet
Birds singing in the tall trees
Flowers swaying gently in the breeze
Distributing their incense
Fresh air filling my lungs
That's what happiness is!

Gemma Miles (13)
Whitchurch High School, Cardiff

The Millennium Stadium

The Millennium Stadium is not a rugby or football stadium,
To me it is a turtle laying helplessly on its back,
Its legs dangling tiredly in the air,
25 tiny ants crawling on their stomachs and another
72,000 cheering as Earnie nets the ball,
Like the turtle hasn't eaten, the turtle's stomach rumbles loudly,
Then it settles down again until
90 minutes finishes.

Nick Bond (12)
Whitchurch High School, Cardiff

The Moon And The Stars

At the sea, the dusk set, with
The sea shining upon the moon
The moon gazed down at the seafront
As the cluttered shells danced
Along the seashore, and the pebbles bashed.
As the tide came in,
The sun set and the day was over.

Emma Gill (11)
Whitchurch High School, Cardiff

Excitement

It's a sense of invisibility you can't explain,
You would give anything to feel it again.

It tastes so bitter, sweet and sour,
Like pollen and incense rising from a flower.

It's loud and upfront,
It bellows in my ear,
It gives me a lick,
But gives me no fear.

It feels so soft, smooth as well,
A velvet touch, a silver bell.

This emotion is excitement, you've probably guessed,
This feeling is incredible, it's by far the best!

Jack Butler (13)
Whitchurch High School, Cardiff

Anger

It's like fire burning inside you,
It's like thumping in your head.
It's like lightning striking above you,
It's like the colours black and red.

It's like nails scratching a whiteboard,
It's like the smell of rotten eggs.
It's like knives digging inside you,
Stop it please! I beg.

It's like evil eyes staring at you,
Waiting for you to explode.
You hear ringing in your ears,
Is your mind about to implode?

Sophie Davies (13)
Whitchurch High School, Cardiff

To Those Less Fortunate

The room -
it is square and plain,
the doors are brown and tatty,
they look as if they're going to fall off.
The lights -
are as bright as the sun,
they are all in rows.
The children -
they are sitting quietly.
'Could you help me please!'
she says.
'Of course,' says someone else.
She pushed back in her chair,
the chair squawked along the floorboards.
The walls -
they are dirty,
they have all scratches and marks on them.

Ceri Davenport (12)
Whitchurch High School, Cardiff

Free

I want to be free,
To run along the lush green grass,
To splash among the waves of the sea,
And see the golden sunset last.

I want to be free,
To feel the air of the wind on my face,
To taste the honey made by the bee,
And run so fast that my heart does race.

I want to be free.

I want to be free.

Robyn Pesticcio (13)
Whitchurch High School, Cardiff

Unrequited Love

I am the curtain blocking out the light,
When light descends I'm darkness,
In morning, I am night.
I am the winter when the sun is beaming,
The cold breath you exhale,
The nightmare when you're dreaming.
I am the broken mirror, hung from a rusty hook,
I am the torn pages in a dusty book.
I am the silent assassin, shooting hope down in your head,
Tearing up your ego, cutting the last thread.

You are the bittersweet shriek inside my mind,
You are self-hate masked in lust,
You're presence left behind,
You're anonymous, but I identify,
You are the crave I love to hate,
You're the crack cut in the sky,
You are never, but somehow eternity,
You are a wound that never seems to heal forever,
You're invisible, but I notice you appear,
You're a burden, a satanic nemesis,
That remains ever dear.

We're nothing but an emotion,
You experience but never hold,
Hard with a liquid centre,
So hot, yet so ice-cold.
We've embroidered on the canvas,
That's pinned under your skin,
Tainting your insides, we're lurking, deep within.
We are the scream that you always hear,
We're the sour taste upon your tongue,
The ringing in your ear.

I am the curtain sewn onto your heart,
You are the hidden feeling that breaks my life apart.

Harriet Jones (13)
Whitchurch High School, Cardiff

Love

A bright white light,
A heavenly room,
The taste of strawberry lipgloss,
The smell of roses all in bloom.
I hear the sound of singing angels as he's walking up the drive,
I'm feeling wings of excitement fluttering inside,
I hope this feeling never ends,
I want to jump, I want to sing,
Now I know we're more than friends.

Lois Jeremy (13)
Whitchurch High School, Cardiff

Hate

Like being balanced on a knife's edge,
The black pupil of your eye,
The little girl on a window ledge,
Staring up to the sky,
As love and peace begin to fall,
You hear screams of pain,
Trapped by a purple wall,
Only hate shall remain.

Holly Venus (14)
Whitchurch High School, Cardiff

Star

He is standing on the light green grass,
with sounds every second of time.
He is celebrating from a lovely goal from a layoff shot.
Brown hair like a light brown bear,
eyes like the sun always catches my eye,
everywhere I walk.
Blue is like him,
never stops and always changing direction.

Phillip Kavanagh (13)
Whitchurch High School, Cardiff

The River

The river twists around,
Getting faster and faster with every passing second.
It is enclosed in a never-ending tunnel.
The air is cold, still, empty.
The river is wild,
Sweeping everything in its way into the blackness ahead.
The river of my heart.

The harsh, icy water cuts into the sides of the tunnel,
Until it is vast, huge, titanic.
Eventually the river slows,
But it's still there.
Unlike him,
He's gone.
Never to be seen again.
The river,
The river of my heart.

Harriet Tangney (13)
Whitchurch High School, Cardiff

My Mum

She's in a place where there are lots of people
People in bed
Ill people
People who come to visit

She is talking a lot
She makes sure there are beds for people
She cares

She's got brown hair
Shortish
She has a violet top on
She is yellow
She's always happy
Smiling.

Charlotte Culliford (12)
Whitchurch High School, Cardiff

Late Night Granny In A Red Dress

When I'm old I will dress in red,
Wear big clacky high heels
And fall over and hit my head.
I'll be a hip old granny who parties every night
And I'll never go home without a fight.
I will get a big house and sleep in every day,
Go to work and resign
And go to the cinema with popcorn and wine.

I'll live my life freely, do whatever I want,
Live through my life until I'm fed up.
I will smell like my grandma,
The one who smells really nice.
You have to look after the environment too,
So I'll plant a pomegranate down the loo.

But now I'm getting bored of you,
Get out of my house or I'll shove you down the loo.
So tell your kids the story I have told you,
And tell them to be a cool granny . . . before 2004!

Rebecca Ann Woodfield (11)
Whitchurch High School, Cardiff

Hallowe'en!

It's that time again.
It's Hallowe'en,
Time to dress with a horror theme.
Masks, capes, broomsticks too,
How you dress, it's up to you.
Knocking on doors,
Trick or treating,
Lots of candy and sweets for eating.
Ghosts and ghouls,
A night of fear,
But there again,
It's only once a year!

Danielle Evans (12)
Whitchurch High School, Cardiff

My Little Brother

The place is nice and big.
Tap is running.
Someone is on the Xbox.
He is laughing
at the colour of my room.
Plain.
He is playing on the Xbox.
Then suddenly he jumps on my bed
kicks me
he is in a bad mood
because he lost.
He looks as if he's just been fighting
in the mud
with pigs.
He smells
horrible
like a drain.
He has blue eyes like a pool of water
smallish ears.
He reminds me of the colour blue.
When it rains
he's normally not in a mood.
He also reminds me of the colour yellow because he is normally happy
sometimes.

Joshua Yanez (12)
Whitchurch High School, Cardiff

Witches

W itches live in spooky castles.
 I n the castle they make potions
 T o turn people into toads, frogs and bats,
 C hanting words that humans would never think of
 H aunting the sky at witching hour.
 E ach witch has a black cat.
 S caring people is what witches like to do.

Rhiannon Lavin (12)
Whitchurch High School, Cardiff

To Those Less Fortunate

In the room
it is white walls like plain paper
a rusty cupboard in the back
like rust off a bike
a table top made of wood
and sky-blue.
A person said,
'Get out of my room.'
'No, I don't want to.'
'Just get out.'
The person walked
away when the chair
thundered to the floor
and the door slammed shut.
It sounded like
a rock hit the ground
pictures in the back of
the room
notice board at the front
and a storage door
and it is as blue as the sea.
The windows like ice
light as bright as full beam
on a car.
The floor is as beige
as a jumper.
When you look out
of the ice windows
you see rooftops.

Leigh Jenkins (12)
Whitchurch High School, Cardiff

Zombies' Night

Spooky nights
Freaky sights make you shiver
Creaky noises
Bone-chilling spells
Evil smells fill the air

Spooky nights
Blood-sucking nights - frightened
Creaky
Spooky nights

Darkness falls, shadow moves
Dreadful, bleak
Screeching claw
Makes you terrified.

Mark Raicis (12)
Whitchurch High School, Cardiff

My Sister

She's in her bedroom
Pink wallpapered walls
Black TV
Staring her in the face
Laughing to herself
Sitting down on her bed
Like a swan
Brushing her red auburn hair
Eyes glistening
She is like a rare lilac rose
She can hear the wind
Whistling outside
As children get carried
Down the road.

Kelly Batchelor (12)
Whitchurch High School, Cardiff

The Classroom

It sounds like a big room with lots of things in it.
I can feel lots of strange things.
I can hear creaking noises along the narrow path.
I can hear noises outside like cars going by.
I can feel moving objects with something thin in their hands
And something thick on something smooth -
Also I can feel four long things sticking in the ground.
I walk over to a window with something really hard.
I try to push it, it slings open, the air blows in my face,
I can hear noises from all directions.
I turn back round, run my hand across the cold wall,
I hit something, it's cold and very smooth with something in front of it.
I could feel lots of heavy things and lots of thin things around.
I had an idea I was in a school in a classroom.

Lewis Davies (12)
Whitchurch High School, Cardiff

The Reflection

Look into the water, there you are,
a small child playing on the bank.

You go home, run up the stairs,
in the mirror is a larger boy.

Sitting there, gazing out of the window
you see yourself, a middle-aged man.

Walking through the park you throw bread for the ducks,
the water shows an old man on the bank.

You go home, walk up the stairs
and in the mirror is an ancient man.

You look down through the clouds, you see the oldest man
you've ever seen lying in his own coffin.

Lloyd Davies (12)
Whitchurch High School, Cardiff

The Coolest Granny Ever!

When I am old,
I will be very bold.
I will live in Venice,
And be a bit of a menace!

My scent will be musky,
And I will have a pet husky.
My fashion sense will be wise,
And I will win a good looks prize!

I will drive my Ferrari, the snazziest in town,
I will drive it so fast that I won't be able to frown!
As an old woman I will be very cool,
And every day I shall swim in my indoor pool!

And that is why I will be the coolest granny ever!

Ruby Jones (11)
Whitchurch High School, Cardiff

The Devil

There it is, glaring at me,
His corrupt eyes burning in anger,
His nose twitching with frustration,
His blood-red face bubbling and boiling with sheer evil.
He launched his pronged fork into the distance,
And roared with all his might!
It was as if there was boiling lava streaming in his eyeballs!
He was still staring eye to eye with me,
I am standing shakily trying to wipe out my fear.
He bellowed my name,
Sweat dripping all over me,
I am in Hell forever!

Elliott Jones (12)
Whitchurch High School, Cardiff

The Enchanted Sea

I felt as if the sea was a twister
As it tosses and turns
It sticks out like a blister
It never goes away
The sea comes to life
And dances roughly
It pirouettes in the air
You cannot see a thing
I call it
I sit and the day goes by
I stare out to sea
You feel as if you could fly
When you stare at the sea
The waves clash
Together as one
It makes a bashing sound
You hear voices from the sea
The sun beams on the sand
And makes a print
I hear a mythical band
But don't know where.

Victoria Grainger (11)
Whitchurch High School, Cardiff

My Pet Dog

M izzie is the name of the dog that I own,
Y ou usually see her chewing on a big, juicy bone.

P eople often stop,
E veryone stares,
T o catch a glimpse of her beautiful hair.

D igging up the garden,
O ften I will call,
G ood girl Mizzie, there goes the ball.

Will Morris (12)
Whitchurch High School, Cardiff

School

Sometimes school can be OK,
You have to go anyway.

Boring writing, boring sums,
PE, art, textiles,
Brilliant fun.

Sometimes school can be OK,
You have to go anyway.

The worst bit is,
I bet you can guess,
The *homework!*
It gets in a mess.

Sometimes school can be OK,
You have to go anyway.

But at the end of the day,
You have to go,
I hate to admit it but . . .
It can be fun you know.

Harriet Rudden (11)
Whitchurch High School, Cardiff

Red

Fierce flickering flames,
Running like a tiger,
Spreading around the world, bold as anger.

Volcanoes erupt,
Flowing lava,
Running violently down the slopes of desire.

Roaring dragons,
Breathe out fire,
Suffocating smoke swirling higher, higher, higher.

Elizabeth Worby (11)
Whitchurch High School, Cardiff

When I Am Old

My hair is grey, what's left of it
My teeth are false
My specs are thick
My legs don't work like they used to
So a wheelchair ride I have to do

I also have a Zimmer frame to move around the floor
A lift to go up the stairs
And a spyhole in my door

I still enjoy a good old chat
With my old pals who share a flat
We go away on OAP trips
And cause a riot with our walking sticks

It's not that bad being old
It could be worse, I could be bald.

David Harrhy (12)
Whitchurch High School, Cardiff

Lost In A House Of Horror

Gloomy shapes fill the room
Screeching, tapping and banging loudly
Blood all over the seats
Dreadful smell
Rooms fill with a spine-chilling silence
Dusty old windows
Stairs tap with misery
Ghosts touch your shoulder while whispering in your ear
Running from the darkness and horror
Smell of death in the lost horror house.

Pauline Parsons (13)
Whitchurch High School, Cardiff

The Mirror

There I was, just sitting there,
With a reflection staring back,
It was on a cold winter's day,
And it happened just like that.

The dust collected layer upon layer,
As the reflection became greyer and greyer,
The mirror shone a sparkling clean,
As the years went past it gleamed a mouldy green.

There I was, just sitting there,
With a reflection staring back,
It was on a cold winter's day,
And it happened just like that.

Rhiannon Jones (12)
Whitchurch High School, Cardiff

The Face In The Water

A smiley face looks back at me.
Who is that there that I can see?
Is there someone behind my back,
Ready to jump out and attack?

I look deeply into her eyes,
I lift my hand up to the skies.
She lifts hers too as if by magic,
Now that didn't feel so tragic!

It's like we're attached by puppet strings,
Like someone's making us do the same things.
Isn't it strange that we're not joined together?
We should be linked together forever!

Rebecca Shelley (13)
Whitchurch High School, Cardiff

As Crazy As Can Be

When I'm old I will be shopping mad,
I'll buy lots of clothes on my credit card,
I'll phone my mates,
And make some cakes,
Go out clubbing on lots of dates.

I'll be as *crazy* as can be,
And no one can possibly stop me,
I'll work in Threshers,
And eat lots of refreshers,
I'll watch TV in the evening,
And eat lots of sweets.

Then snuggle up in bed and say,
'Goodnight!'

Charlotte Marlow (11)
Whitchurch High School, Cardiff

Getting Old

When I'm old I shall do anything I want!
If you think I'm going to be a sweet old lady well you're wrong
I will stay up late
I will call my mate
I will have a dog
I will name it Mog
I will have a cat
I will name it Mat
I'll try to be kind
But you never mind
Because I'll be older than you are and I will do what I want!

Sophie Steele (11)
Whitchurch High School, Cardiff

Skating Granny

When I'm old I'm going to get a house,
And buy a big fat pussycat,
Put jam on the staircase and slide right down,
Then go shopping into town,
My friends told me not to dress like a clown,
But I then decided to go back into town,
Dye my hair pink,
To match my new high heels,
Or maybe I could get some skates with wheels.

Race into the supermarket,
On my way I'll grab a basket,
Zooming through I grab some cheese,
Coffee, tea, carrots and peas,
Plenty of salad with chunks of salami,
Perhaps I might get some pastrami,
To the checkout,
I'm not going to hang about,
Let's jump the queue, that's what I'll do.

With high speed I'll race out the shop,
Oops I forgot the pop!
Get out my way you little kids,
'Corrie' is on the telly,
Now it's time to fill my belly,
It's home time now, I must go home.

Being old isn't that bad,
I never wanted to be old, now I'm glad,
It's fun because I'm super skating granny.

Ellie May Gibbs (12)
Whitchurch High School, Cardiff

How Time Flies!

I looked in the bath,
Time crawled,
I looked in the stream,
Time walked,
I looked at the sea,
Time ran,
I looked in the mirror,
Time flew,
I looked at you and
Time stopped.

I was free as the wind,
Time crawled,
I had friends who loved me,
Time walked,
I left my friends,
Time ran,
I lost my friends,
Time flew,
I lost you,
Time stopped.

Jessica Phillips (12)
Whitchurch High School, Cardiff

Anger

It swells up inside you, fighting to escape,
It won't let go,
Can't stop grasping.
Its evil screech, blurting out without warning.
Its smell of rancid fish, so intoxicating, turning your moist nostrils dry.
It feels coarse and irregular,
Making you gag on touch,
Anger is the thing that you hate so much.

Gareth Bodman (14)
Whitchurch High School, Cardiff

Old And At The Pool

When I'm old I will go to the pool,
And splash everyone by jumping in,
I'll go down the slippery slide,
And be as noisy as sin.

When I do my 16 lengths,
It'll be easy I should think,
But after the 20 minute swim,
You will see my face so pink.

I'll wear blue bathers,
And bring my goggles, they're blue,
Although I'm over 70,
I will make the most, will you?

Amy Richards (11)
Whitchurch High School, Cardiff

When I Ride

When I am old I will buy a Harley Davidson.
I will race all the other grandpas I meet
And wake up all the babies in the street.
I will get a Subaru
And race it through all the streets
And hopefully get a few beats.
I'm going to parachute
One thousand feet
And amaze the people I meet.
I will jump to Mars
On a trampoline made of stars
And hopefully be home for tea.

Ben Popek (11)
Whitchurch High School, Cardiff

Sonnet Of Love

My boyfriend's eyes are much colder than ice
His hair's as real as silicone implants
The bent shape of his teeth is far from nice
Creeps up your nerves like poison ivy plants

His skin has more boils than an old kettle
Lips are as brittle as a frozen twig
The words he speaks are sharp as a nettle
The clothes he wears makes him look like a pig

A nose as deformed as Quasimodo
How could he evade his terrible smell
The sound of his voice is the worst I've known
The amount in his head's very hard to tell

But however bad my boyfriend may seem
Our love is unbroken, just him and me.

Bethan Salaman (14)
Whitchurch High School, Cardiff

Untitled

Her lungs are as skinny as twigs found on the floor
She runs like a hippo with sleeping tablets,
Her voice is as loud as a huge, wild boar,
Her hair is as shiny as intestines and guts,
She eats like a pig that's been starved for 8 days,
She dances like a rhino with its feet covered in cuts,
Her skin is so pale, she's been starved of the sun's rays,
Her brain is so small it closely resembles a moth,
She writes like a 5-year-old with Parkinson's,
She smells like a skunk who's had the fright of its life,
Her breath is so cold it would make you *run, run, run*,
Her touch is so hard it's like being stabbed by a knife,
Though I wouldn't leave her 'cause she is mine after all,
And she doesn't laugh at me when I hit the floor!

Christopher Nukes (14)
Whitchurch High School, Cardiff

My Prince Charming

My prince's heart pounds like a beating jungle drum,
With hair taut and tense as the strings of a violin,
His voice is as loud and harsh as a trumpet will ever become,
And his nose sprays so wide, I think there's a tuba within.

His eyes are so mean that no shimmer can be found,
His lips are so callous like a gruesome old trout,
His ears are gigantic like balloons flying around,
And his teeth are as big as a colossal pig's snout.

I hate it when his bum wriggles like a playful baboon,
And the way he loves himself like a made-up drag queen,
He always strives for attention whenever he walks into a room,
And the eyes of my prince are as dark as Hell's ever been.

However much I hate him his love is a dart,
And nobody but my prince will ever be in my heart.

Hanna Brunt (14)
Whitchurch High School, Cardiff

Sonnet

My boyfriend's eyes are as lifeless as death,
His hair is so greasy like a chip pan,
Rancid and sick is the smell of his breath,
He is the most dullest, stupidest man.
He's as scruffy and dirty as a tramp,
His voice sounds like nails scratching a blackboard,
His clothes smell musty and of rising damp,
He's full of himself but it leaves me bored.
His teeth are as rotten as a dead corpse,
His repulsive face is ugly as Hell,
His stare goes straight through me, just like a hawk's,
He suffers from gruesome acne as well.
Although he's controlled by the TV screen,
One that I love more, there has never been.

Joanna Cawley (14)
Whitchurch High School, Cardiff

Teachers

Teachers shout at you,
They always do,
They are always shouting,
'Detention, detention,
Pay attention.'

They give us a load of school work,
But they still give us homework.

When we play a good game,
They are always the same,
They ban the game and say it's too rough,
So now we play boring old touch.

The best part of the day,
Is when the teachers all go away,
And we all run home for another day.

Fred Rowlands (11)
Whitchurch High School, Cardiff

Is This Our World?

The wind howls like a wild wolf,
The sky swallows the world with
Its dull black cloak,
The animals run for shelter from
This cacophonous storm.
The trees sway and tremble with fear,
The cars skate along polluted roads,
We hurt ourselves and damage our bodies,
There is no green and not any forests.
Is this our world?

Megan Poley (11)
Whitchurch High School, Cardiff

When I'm Old!

When I'm an old granny
I will go out in my slippers
And walk slowly across the road
I am not going to marry an old toad
I will travel the world and see lots of things
I will wear bright clothes
And smell like a rose
When I turn old.

I will have a walking stick
And hit people with it
When I am old, scary and bold
I will probably turn into mould
I will drink lots of tea
And add lots of sugar for me
To boost my blood pressure
And it will *explode!*

Bryony Acton (11)
Whitchurch High School, Cardiff

I'm A . . . ?

I'm fast but not a hare.
I can grow very big but I start small
I like surfers, I can smell you a mile away if you bleed.
I hunt in packs or on my own.
I'm known as great and I'm known as white,
But I'm a dark blue, I live in the sea.
I can eat a man whole but I prefer fish.
I have seven rows of razors
I'm a great white shark.

James Copner (12)
Whitchurch High School, Cardiff

Granny D

When I'm old,

I'll go out partying every night,
And not dare leave till I've seen a fight!
I'll go into restaurants and be really rude
By purposely moaning about the food.

I'll go into town in one of my flash cars
And have fun in the clubs and bars.
I'll shop like mad for things that don't suit,
Like bright pink bags and snakeskin boots!

I'll go on holiday to Disneyland,
And come off the rides unable to stand,
I'll go to Ascot on ladies' day,
And cheer on the horses as they gallop away!

The times I'll have will be great fun,
But for the time being I'll enjoy being young!

Bethan Delve (11)
Whitchurch High School, Cardiff

Old And Mouldy

When I am old I shall go out in the rain,
and everyone will think that I'm insane.
When I am old I will be very small,
and always ignore all of my calls.
When I am old I will be very cold,
and all my food will be covered in mould.
When I am old I shall stay in all day,
and not go out for work or play.
When I am old and can't go very far,
I will no longer be able to drive my car.
When I am old and enjoy a nice nap,
sitting by the fire with my cat on my lap.

Jessica Puttick (11)
Whitchurch High School, Cardiff

The Vampire

As the sun got pulled down
By the dark and gloomy night
A vampire crept out of his grave.

He roamed the city looking for prey.
As he wandered the empty streets of a helpless city
He found himself an open window.

He went over to the open window and looked in
There lay a young lady silently enjoying her sleep.
But she did not know she could not enjoy it anymore.

The vampire crept quietly into the lonely bedroom
Leant over the young lady
And started to breathe heavily.

As he sunk his rotten, pointy teeth
Into her velvet soft skin,
He sunk deeply into her veins.

He pulled his teeth away from the young girl's neck
Licked every last drop of blood from her neck
Then licked his lips as the taste of blood thrilled him.

He was now full and could not feast on any more blood.
He then left the quiet and empty room
And crept once again across the gloomy city.

As the sun rose from the dark clouds
The vampire swiftly crept back
Into his tomb!

Sophie Jones (12)
Whitchurch High School, Cardiff

Treasures On The Beach

I went to the beach
When the tide was out
Where pretty treasures lay all about
Something glistened, was it a pearl
Or maybe even a mermaid's curl?

Sandcastles stand all alone
Amongst some rubbish and an ice cream cone
Not a soul in sight
It was nearly night
The sea looked calm
But it can do such harm

All I wanted was you next to me
To see the things that I could see
As the beach brings so much pleasure
Amongst its hidden treasure.

Siân Jones (12)
Whitchurch High School, Cardiff

My Grandad

My grandad sits in his rocking chair,
Mourning over the loss of his hair.
He rocks back and forth, then falls to sleep,
The snoring so loud, like a lion; so deep.
His false teeth scare me as they're going green,
Why doesn't Granny give them a clean?
He trundles about on his electric scooter,
If you annoy him he honks on his hooter!
He always complains and his joints are all sore,
His knees creak like an old wooden door.
He's always exclaiming 'this day and age is bad',
And tells long stories of when he was a lad.
Though all he does is moan and groan,
To me he's still a king on his throne!

Laura Phelan (12)
Whitchurch High School, Cardiff

The Haunted Castle!

In a haunted castle
I was all alone.
My heart pounded. It was dark inside the castle.
There were weird noises.
A door opened silently,
No one was there.
I walked into a room with a dining table and chairs.
There was something on the table.
I walked to it, I went to touch it but I heard someone scream.
I could not feel my legs. My blood felt like hot boiling lava.
I went to see who it was that screamed, I looked everywhere,
But there was no one.

There was a mirror right in front of me, I looked at it,
And there was something coming behind me.
I turned around, I looked at it then fell to the floor and
Blanked out, it was dark.

Frankie Self (13)
Whitchurch High School, Cardiff

F.A.T.

My love's eyes are like prunes chewed by a dog,
She's shaped like a plum, best seen in thick fog.
When she talks, she spits like a hard-ass thug,
Her too-podgy nose is shaped like a plug.
Her teeth are as crooked as a pensioner's hip,
She's as stupid as a witch who needs a good kip.
Her chin is creased like an old man's behind,
My love's hair is wild; the least tidy you'll find.
She smells like soiled pants, just left to rot,
She sings like a cat with a major blood clot.
Her lips are as crusty as a half-picked scab,
Her breasts as loose as socks filled up with sand.
Everyone questions her vile face,
But how can I fault her true inner grace?

Adam Jones (14)
Whitchurch High School, Cardiff

Sonnet #1 - The Original

His eyes refuse to glisten like the midday sun,
And Sahara rock would offer more comfort than his lips,
I believe the fullest moon is more discreet than his bum,
As its width offers a larger area than a pregnant woman's hips.
His voice is as harsh as horseradish sauce,
And his nose is reminiscent of the most crooked parsnip,
Hair as straggly as the tail of a horse,
And so greasy I wish not to know in what it has been dipped!
My love's ears are grotesque, large and unsyringed,
With teeth as mangled as a rabbit stuck in barbed wire,
It is simply enough to make one cringe,
And his laugh - more like a crackle of a well-lit fire.

Hearing all of this you think I would stray
But his love, his soul, his charm are more than enough
                                        to make me stay.

Ellie Barrow (14)
Whitchurch High School, Cardiff

Sonnet

My boyfriend's eyes are no deep, endless pit
His voice isn't smooth like a polished dance floor
His sense of humour is not of great wit
His skin's not as gold as sand on the shore
My boyfriend's looks aren't the best that I've seen
If lips are rosy then his are not rare
He stands far too tall for the age fourteen
His normal hands aren't the softest of pairs
My boyfriend is not amazingly smart
His teeth aren't perfect and no way pearl-white
He talks with his brain and not with his heart
When he hugs me he doesn't hold me tight
My boyfriend's qualities seem bad and yet
I thank the heavens and stars that we met!

Helena Reid (14)
Whitchurch High School, Cardiff

Night-Time

Dusty grey clouds sail slowly in the sky
and crawl across the room.
A thousand lights hang up in mid-air,
glowing between the darkness.
The breeze is chilling
and bites at the air
and cools the night around.
The world around seems empty
and the silence is cold.
There is no one in the homes around
except the burning candles in the windows
leaving flickering shadows
dancing on the walls.
Creatures so small,
swoop in-between air currents
and leave tiny silhouettes
on the moon's face.

Laura Alice Summerscales (13)
Whitchurch High School, Cardiff

Sonnet I

My boyfriend's stature is not great by any degree,
He is as tall as cut grass and looks vastly out of place.
His greasy, matted hair is not 'cool' even to me,
Vile, muddied worms drizzle over his face.
He does not have sculptured muscles - useful for a fight,
My man is as puissant as a kitten without claws.
Neither has he a smile of resplendent white,
But dirty pebbles grimace from between his jaws.
And my beau's skin is not smooth or golden with tan,
But rather pink, like salmon, in its complexion.
True, never have I seen a live Vitruvian man,
Though my love's semblance is far from angelic perfection.
And yet, I know, that never could I love him more,
If even he possessed no common, earthly flaw.

Lauren Kelly (14)
Whitchurch High School, Cardiff

Reflections On The Inside

People's reflections aren't just what they look like . . .

People that are thin, maybe fat,
Bursting with happiness,
Or maybe they're sad.

They can look in the mirror,
And see what they see,
But in life, they might not feel so free.

But when their life comes to a low,
It will almost definitely come and show,
And if not dealt with,
The problem will grow.

And finally, in their dreams,
They will get reflected flashes,
Until eventually,
The mirror,
Smashes.

Don't be a victim of your own
Reflections, bad times and images,
Deal with them,
Before your life finishes.

Craig Perriam (13)
Whitchurch High School, Cardiff

Girl In My Mirror

There is a girl in my mirror,
She's in there every day,
She copies every move I make,
Each and every way.
When I smile she smiles,
When I frown she frowns,
And then it struck me,
The girl in my mirror,
Is actually me!

Carys Morris (12)
Whitchurch High School, Cardiff

My Dog

There is a red sky.
The sun is disappearing under the sea.
The sand is golden and the tide is creeping closer.
There is nobody around
But the dog in the sea.

The dog is chasing the waves.
When the waves come in she runs away.
I throw the ball into the sea
And the dog goes under.
She comes out and her paws mark the sand.

The dog is small, brown and white.
She has long, brown, dangling ears
And a white stripe between her eyes.
She is slim and quite short.
She has energy waiting to burst.

If I had to give my dog a colour
It would be yellow,
Because she's always happy and cheerful.
She is loyal, obedient and very sensible.
She is very young and always ready to play.

The cliffs are high
And there are sheep grazing.
The dog is looking at the sheep.
There are some surfers
But the waves aren't high enough
The water is very still.

Vanessa Hayden (11)
Whitchurch High School, Cardiff

The Warrior

From the shadow of the forest he comes,
Cape wiping in the wind,
His steed pure white in the moonlight,
Helmet sat proudly on his head.

His sword at his hip,
And shield on his back,
His armour strong and beautiful,
He stands ready.

And from behind him emerge a thousand men,
All ready for battle,
All ready for their fate,
All ready for war.

He draws his sword
And with that his men shout to the heavens,
All shouting for their loved ones,
All shouting for victory.

Then silence . . .

The warrior dismounts and steps forward,
In his sword lies the strength of his country,
And in his heart lies their faith.
He stands ready.

Jacob Tucker (14)
Whitchurch High School, Cardiff

Your Name

I wrote your name in the sky,
    the wind blew it away,
I wrote your name in the sand,
    the sea washed it away,
I wrote your name in my heart
    and forever it will stay.

James Kelly (12)
Whitchurch High School, Cardiff

The Raven And The Seagull

Said the raven to the seagull,
'I believe that you are new.'
'Yes,' replied the seagull,
'I come from Timbuktu.'

'Timbuktu,' said the raven,
'That is so far away.'
'Yes,' replied the seagull,
'I almost lost my way.'

'Lost your way?' said the raven,
'Now how did you do that?'
'Well,' replied the seagull,
'I quite forgot my map!'

'Forgot your map!' said the raven,
'When will seagulls learn?'
'Well,' replied the seagull,
'I took a wrong left turn.'

'Well,' said the raven,
'I've had quite enough of you.'
'So?' replied the seagull,
'You're pretty boring too!'

Isabelle Pettersson (12)
Whitchurch High School, Cardiff

Love Is Like A Mirror

Love can blind you,
Like a mirror in the sun,
It can be slightly cracked,
When it's broken, the pieces are like a puzzle,
Hard to fix back,
When overcrowded it's difficult to see,
Then when everything is gone you realise,
Love was made for you and me.

Tenesiha Allen (13)
Whitchurch High School, Cardiff

Golden Tears

Golden tears drain your soul
The painful cry rots your mind
Mirrors cascading round me
The gateway to happiness is always open

My mind is frozen
My heart turns to stone
Everyone around me stops like a break in time
There is no colour shining down on the land

The Earth revolves around the luminous sun while
My breath is on fire
As the tear runs down the edge of the smooth round face
The light in the reflection of my life lit up

The happiness opens out of the bright smile
The twinkle of the eye watches around
The gateway of happiness is always open.

Claire Nokes (12)
Whitchurch High School, Cardiff

My Mum's Wonderful Day

My mum watching TV in the front room,
lying on the sofa with the brightly patterned
wallpaper all around her.

She is watching Neighbours, eating her dinner,
drinking her tea and talking to me
and my sister.

She has blonde hair, she's not tall,
she wears a dress and black boots,
her favourite colour is purple and most of her tops are purple.

If my mum was a colour she would be violet
because the plant is beautiful and so is my mum.

In my garden my two guinea pigs are running around
and munching on the green wavy grass.

Gareth Jones (11)
Whitchurch High School, Cardiff

The Reflection Of The Mirror

In comes Mother, as usual, plastering herself in paint,
She comes in first as she goes to work and doesn't want to be late.

Now it's turn for Father, smothering himself in lather,
He's a regular guest, just in his vest
As he always wants to look his best.

Oh no, look who's coming, spotty teenager on her way,
I close my eyes and get a surprise as something splats my face!

Now it's time for little brother, he looks nothing like his ugly mother,
Why's he standing pulling funny faces?
He's putting his fingers in unusual places!

I sit here in the bathroom, every night and every day,
If you were to take this job you wouldn't be satisfied as it provides
                                                                no pay.
When everyone has gone, I sit and reflect on how people
                              would react if I had *my* say.

Sara Bodger (12)
Whitchurch High School, Cardiff

Your Life

You advance into the maze
The sharp sun pounding brightly off the Lilliputian round mirrors
The white blinding you like a bottle of still water
Your watch shining illustrious silver like a suit of armour
                                        and beating like a drum
Everything shining in your life suddenly concussed away
                    into darkness like a mournful drawer
Then your water spills and is empty
At the end your watch cracks and stops drumming like a boxer falling.

Harrison Jankovic (12)
Whitchurch High School, Cardiff

When Will Morning Come?

It's dark and silent apart from the hooting of the owls outside.
Your mind is playing tricks on you.
It feels like morning will never come.
You sit alone, hoping that it will.

You see images of ghosts but you know inside that they are only
                                                                            the curtains.
The wardrobes are making scary shadows on the floor.
The eyes in the pictures are following you.
When will morning come?

You hear a door creaking and a tiptoe up the stairs.
You are ready to fight, ready to scare away the intruder,
When suddenly the bedroom door opens and it's Mum
                                                                            home from work.
You are relieved when the light is turned on and everything
                                                                        is back to normal.

Rachel Seary (12)
Whitchurch High School, Cardiff

My Girl

She looks as pleasing as a pug dog which has been slapped by a fish,
Her ears flap like an elephant tail on double ecstasy,
She smells as putrid as a pig in an outbreak of cholera,
She walks like a hippopotamus with constipation,
She's as fat as a whale which has been in McDonald's for a week.,
Her sight is like a blind monkey in a rubbish bag,
Her eyes are as bulging as a frog's throat with elastication,
She speaks like a foghorn which has been on helium,
Her skin is as harsh as a brick wall which has been through a storm,
She swims like a fat bear on a unicycle,
Her teeth are as wonky as a drunk mandrill with three legs,
She sings like a car exhaust with its silencer nicked,
Yet my word she can't half cook,
So I don't really care how she may look.

Joe Farmer (14)
Whitchurch High School, Cardiff

My Lifetime Of My Nan

I'm waiting on the stairs,
Waiting for my nan to leave the living room,
In the living room there are photos, cupboards and wonderful colours,
On the floor there is laminate flooring.

As I was waiting for my nan I went to the toilet,
My nan asked for help,
But I was too late.

Red books fell on her head,
But she was OK.

My nan has white curly hair,
She looks kind,
She is wearing her work clothes because
She had not long got back from cleaning the workshop.

If I had to choose a colour I would choose bright yellow,
Because she is kind and whenever I see her she gives me money.

Chris Kavanagh (11)
Whitchurch High School, Cardiff

My Dad's Perfect Day

My dad's watching TV in the living room on the sofa,
just dozing off slowly, my living room is brightly coloured
with a couple of pictures on the walls.

My dad is racing his motorbike with all his friends,
but as usual he was losing because he cannot ride as fast
as his friends because he is scared to go as fast.

My dad is quite short, he is shorter than all his friends,
he has quite dark brown coloured hair and he likes to play football
and he coaches my football team.

He would be a yellow because he can be mostly cheerful
but he can be moody so he would be a red colour.

It is a sunny, happy day where the sun is shining
and there are a couple of clouds in the bright blue sky.

Adam Joslin (11)
Whitchurch High School, Cardiff

Wave

I lie on my board,
Paddle out to sea,
Salt in my face,
Sand in my teeth,
I feel the rush of the wind in my hair,
Dolphins leaping everywhere.

I see the wave coming,
I know what to do,
Stand up on my board,
Look at the blue.
It roars up behind me, like a lion to its prey,
People stood watching me, back on the bay.

I feel the lift,
It has me in its claw,
I'll take it in my stride,
Till it hits the shore.
I do a few tricks, going left, going right,
I feel I could do this all day, all night.

Feet stretched out wide,
Arms in the air,
Roaring to the beach,
With the wind in my hair,
Making every turn, moving with ease,
Suddenly going, very weak at the knees.

I'm thrown on the beach,
Wave dies to a ripple,
Board by my side,
Backwash seems to tickle.
Get up from the sand,
Step out from the shore,
Paddle back out, to try and catch more!

Caroline Nieuwenhuis (13)
Whitchurch High School, Cardiff

My Mum

She is standing in the kitchen
She is standing and smiling.
The room is small but very tidy.

She is washing up,
She looks like she is rushing.
She finishes,
She starts to tidy up.

She has brown eyes,
Brown hair,
Quite tall.

She reminds me of yellow,
This is because yellow is fresh and brand new.
All of her clothes look brand new and fresh.

This is my mum!

Dave Trace (13)
Whitchurch High School, Cardiff

Witch!

Death challenges you as you approach those woods,
Twisted, deadly that describes them best.
What lurks upon them is supernatural.

A witch. I tell you!
A black hat, scatty dressed witch.
A nose like a bloody knife,
Eyes like red marbles and teeth like . . .
Yellow needles, rotten and sharp.
A mouth that chants those spells.

Dancing around the cauldron
Singing, floating upon the full crusty moon.
She grabs her broomstick and off she goes.

Lauren Brobin (12)
Whitchurch High School, Cardiff

Anger

Why is it so strong?
Why is it the emotion humans are most vulnerable to succumb to?
During the state of mind when one is angry, it is impossible to think of anything other than revenge.
It wells up inside you, burning like a flame until you hear those little voices in your ear,
'Go on! Look what they did to you! They deserve this!'
the little Satan whispers.
His provocations and accusations flood into your ear until they persuade you.
This is what they deserve! They need this to put them in their place!
The demon in your ear hops from you in your blind rage, releasing you from anger.
What have you done? Are they crying? Bleeding? Seething with anger as you once were?
Anger never dies, it either buries inside you, or you remove it from yourself onto others.
Think about this, and next time you're angry, remember what I have taught you, and try to slay that parasitic demon that has infiltrated your psyche . . .

Tom Coates (13)
Whitchurch High School, Cardiff

Friends

A friend is like a flower
A rose to be exact
A friend is like a brand new gate
That never comes unlatched,
A friend is like a spirit
A spirit that never dies
A friend is like a bodyguard
That never says goodbye!

Michelle Escott (14)
Whitchurch High School, Cardiff

A Stroll In The Park

As I stroll down the icy paths in the chilly park
I see that the sky is going dark.
The tall, frosted trees sway freely
It is quite breezy.
Their branches are dull and bare,
But don't worry this isn't rare.
It happens all the time; they'll grow new ones by summer with the sun
But I think summer is too hot, winter is much more fun.
I feel a raindrop
Or maybe it was a snowdrop.
The tiny delicate snowdrops fall
Flooding the path with a fluffy white substance covering all
This is called snow
Which many people love and know.
I see children making shapes in the snow
And chucking snowballs to and fro
Snowmen with scarves and hats are a popular choice to be made
But after a while they melt where they got laid.
Into the snow they disappear
Children want them to reappear
But it's too late now, spring is here
With leaves on trees growing near.

Christina Lago (15)
Whitchurch High School, Cardiff

Winter

Fresh-fallen snow, untouched by man,
nestles itself all around.
The cold, gusty wind, blows in and
out the hollows,
icicles hang like shimmering daggers.
From trees where leaves once hung.
Frosted breath and ice-cold fingertips,
in the long, dark nights of winter.

Michael Lee (16)
Whitchurch High School, Cardiff

Leeds

He is standing in the changing room,
Telling the players the formation set.
The smell of Deep Heat adds to the tension.
He looks at the Leeds badge for the last time
Before leaving the changing room.
The heightened tension and the anxious walk
Down the dark tunnel of Elland Road,
Becomes a proud and emotional time,
For the blue-eyed, grey-haired old man.
The entrance to the sunbeamed stadium
Becomes a dream come true.
The Leeds' manager applauded
The support of the Leeds fans
And kissed the badge that was on his suit.
The yellow, white and blue of Leeds
Reminded the fans of who they have supported
Since they were five years of age.

Nathan Ashley (14)
Whitchurch High School, Cardiff

The Game

Trying to finish the last level,
The game of 'Dawn of the Devil'.
Trying to earn an imaginary medal,
Trying to finish the last level.

All he does is play and play,
All of the time through the day.
People passing as they may,
All he does is play and play.

Starting to hallucinate,
He is starting to think he's great.
Using a computer as a cape,
Starting to hallucinate.

Alex Foley (13)
Whitchurch High School, Cardiff

My First Love

She is standing in my room
Smiling at me
And my room is a nice light blue and quiet.
She is really happy, standing
And looking at my stuff.
She has long blonde hair,
Brown eyes, and a really nice figure.
She is quite shy.
She reminds me of red.
She has red cheeks.
It's really windy outside,
Cars rushing past to go home
Away from the horrible weather.
She's the colour red burning my body
If she comes any closer, I will explode.

Rhys James (13)
Whitchurch High School, Cardiff

Rugby Pitch

He is standing on the pitch
With the ball in his hands
The wind blowing his hair side to side.
His name is Maurice, he is my uncle.
He is on the floor getting rucked over,
Then he gets up and puts his thumb up
And cheers on the rest of the team.
His hair is like coal. He is crazy.
No matter what happens he is always smiling,
In good times and bad.
The wind is getting wild and it starts raining,
But he always says that rain clears his mind.

Jermaine Thompson (13)
Whitchurch High School, Cardiff

Remind Me When October Begins

Whoever liked September anyway?
Green turns to brown
and blue turns to grey.

The rain begins to pound my head,
as the school gates open
and summer is long dead.

The nights inside are boring,
as the work piles up
and the birds no longer sing.

No rest for the labourers,
as holidays are absent
and a long wait till Christmas.

My sleep is long but restless,
as I wait patiently for the future.
Remind me when October begins.

Chris Williams (15)
Whitchurch High School, Cardiff

The Mysterious Park!

The mysterious park was sombre and dark
And the playground was deserted and empty,
Its stern, damaged swings squeaked in the darkness
And its end was near because of the story that found it,
The slide was crooked and twisted
And its hill was like a volcano about to erupt,
Until one strange boy visited this park
And told his friends about it,
Then one day a vast herd of children arrived
At the doorstep and called it The Park of Dreams.

Peter Edward Hughes (11)
Whitchurch High School, Cardiff

My Nan

She's probably sitting in the room right now.
The one in the old people's home.
With her feet up, probably sleeping.
Then she gets woken for a cup of tea.

She blinks as she wakes,
Saying, 'Thank you,' as she receives her tea.
She sips it then starts to talk to me.

She talks softly to me,
I shout a bit,
She can't hear.
I laugh at her
And she laughs back.
She hugs me,
I feel her soft, white hair.

She reminds me of red,
Full of love, joy and happiness.

Rain is lashing down,
She fills the room with warmness.
There's a dog being walked
Looking so happy being wet
In the rain outside.

Charlotte Roberts (13)
Whitchurch High School, Cardiff

The Dolphin

He swam the waves with silky fins;
Near to the coast in rough seas,
Beneath the turquoise waters, twists and turns.

The reefs beneath him crawl,
He watches as creatures brawl,
He quickly vanishes through sea walls.

Chris Harding (14)
Whitchurch High School, Cardiff

My Poem

She is sitting in a room smiling,
It smells like roses.
It has cream walls,
It is very tidy.

She is sitting there
Speaking to her friends.
Her laugh fills the room.

Her brown hair
Is blowing in the wind.
She is wearing a red jumper
And black trousers.

She reminds me of blue
It is her favourite colour.
The walls in her house are blue.

Outside it is quiet
All I can hear is
Children laughing, playing in the park.

Gabby James (13)
Whitchurch High School, Cardiff

The Window

I look out the window,
Rain falls, the window catches it,
Like a teardrop, with a friend to catch it.

I look out the window
Sun shines, the window lets the light in,
Like a smile, with a friend to smile with.

I look out the window,
Snow falls, the window makes a perfect picture,
Like a friendship, with a friend to make the picture perfect.

Rebecca Rhind-Jones (12)
Whitchurch High School, Cardiff

Dad

He is standing behind the bar of an old building
overlooking the water.
The smell of smoke lingers in the air
and the sound of happy people, reverberates around.

Smiling as he pulls a pint,
talking to the customers, happy.

He is going bald,
showing his age,
with a T-shirt and jeans
rippling in the breeze.

He reminds me of blue,
he is always moving,
and changing like the sea.

Outside people bustle around.
The local drunk trips and stumbles.
The water taxi tootles around.

Henry Gidwell (13)
Whitchurch High School, Cardiff

Mum

She is in a hot location
With palm trees all around her,
The cool breeze rushes through
Her golden, blonde hair.
She is relaxed,
Standing still, gazing far away.
She has lovely fair hair
And sky-blue eyes
With shiny white teeth and
Beautiful tanned skin.
She reminds me of the colour blue,
Just like the ocean as it flows calm and peacefully.
Everything around her is still.

Bo Cordle (13)
Whitchurch High School, Cardiff

Amy

She is sitting on a chair.
Baby-blue, dark blue and white pictures on the wall.
Music blaring, others giggling, kind of tidy.
She is singing, laughing and a
Smile is running off her face.
She is just a very happy kind of gal.
Brown hair pulled back into two buns.
Tallish, dark-coloured clothes occasionally.
Bright brown eyes,
Silver ring on her nose,
Shining jewellery in her ears.
She reminds me of yellow
Because she is bright like the sun.
Outside I hear children shouting,
Cars rushing past and
In the distance I hear an ambulance siren.

Emily Chapman (13)
Whitchurch High School, Cardiff

One Spooky Hallowe'en

One spooky Hallowe'en,
I had a party at my house,
Scary, creepy, noisy,
Like a vicious ghost trying to kill me,
Like an axe coming towards me,
It made me feel creepy,
Remember that one Hallowe'en,
Reminds me how scary Hallowe'en can be.

Lauren Fisher (11)
Whitchurch High School, Cardiff

Mum

Pink, blue, purple, warm, bright, comfortable, tidy.
Sitting, smiling, happy reading,
Smells like roses.

Sitting, slow, warm actions.
Smiling, reading, humming a tune.

Tall, think, black thick hair,
Bright, shiny green eyes
With a big smile whatever.

She reminds me of pink because
It's a happy, smiley, bright colour.

Outside it is a hot summer's day
With children laughing outside
With the tune of the ice cream van passing by.

Sinead Heron (13)
Whitchurch High School, Cardiff

The Little Puppy

The little puppy,
Two months old,
Lively, energetic, noisy!
Like a tiny cuddly toy,
As sweet as a sleeping baby,
It makes me feel warm inside,
Like sitting by the fire,
My puppy,
I'll love him forever!

Megan Farmer (11)
Whitchurch High School, Cardiff

Sonnet

His eyes as bright as a solar eclipse
Lashes are clumped from their roots to their tips.
His lips as red as a brown wilting rose
Dying and crying as the sunlight goes.

His voice as smooth as a round red lolly
If dipped in glue and covered in holly.
His hair as soft as a crop of barbed wire
And enough grease to start a chip-pan fire.

Matches are likened to his scrawny arms,
No muscles in sight from shoulder to palm.
His movement is lacking in terms of grace
He's the clumsiest in the human race!

But after all that I have realised
What really matters is on the inside.

Claire Nieuwenhuis (14)
Whitchurch High School, Cardiff

My Life

My life and time, is like an author,
Writing the story of my life,
Each day a new chapter is added,
Chapters just keep adding up and up,
My name carries on and on in each verse,
Paragraph and verse,
We all sit and talk about me and my life yet
No one hardly listens like I'm a solitary spirit in the air.
Daniel, Daniel my name fades on.

Daniel Thomas (13)
Whitchurch High School, Cardiff

A Sonnet

His hair is oily like thick, gloppy glue,
His eyes, shiny brown pools, of which he has two,
His breath smells like disgusting, foul, rotting meat,
It's almost as bad as his two, awfully, smelly feet.

Like a mouse on helium his voice, oh so high,
When he asks if I like it, I just have to lie,
His singing's amazing, it's truly unique,
But like fingers on blackboards, it isn't too sweet.

His legs are as hairy as the hirsute baboon,
I pray to the Lord that he shaves them quite soon.
His toenails are like a cat's needle-sharp claws,
Except so much dirtier, it clogs up his pores.

Yet for all his faults, I love him still,
He's worth it, I know, so ignore them I will!

Jenny Jenkins (14)
Whitchurch High School, Cardiff

Finished

An insect caged, never to be freed,
The eye of Ra as his last colour,
Melts into the never-ending sea of the sky,
The light of the bulb telling you it's ready,
The crisp look of turkey as
It sleeps in the oven.

As the last leaf falls off a tree standing tall.

For everything is finished,
It's time to sleep,
And
Let the blues dance the night away.

Tesni Street (11)
Whitchurch High School, Cardiff

Around The World

I went to France, had some wine
After a few cups, I didn't feel fine.
I went to Spain, and watched a bullfight,
It went on and on all through the night.
I went to Transylvania and met up with Drac'
He was very pale and only wore black.
I went to America and saw the stars,
We went in all the clubs and bars.
I went to Australia and had a koala bear,
He was really cute and had fluffy hair.
I went to Canada and played in the snow,
But someone threw a snowball at me and I was full of woe.
I went to Germany and bought some cheese,
It smelt so bad that it made me sneeze.
I went around the world, but now I'm home,
I would go again but not on my own!

Hannah Lago (12)
Whitchurch High School, Cardiff

My Girlfriend

My girlfriend, so fair and so gentle,
Like an enormous bear being wined and dined.
She talks like a parrot on speed,
And has skin smooth as a rhino's behind.
Her temper needs calming, like a dog on a lead,
Her eyes squint like a mole in a bright light,
She's a face like a toad in the morning,
Which will give you one hell of a fright.
Her hair could be soft and so silky,
But like a badly-groomed horse, needs a brush.
Lips like a chimp badly Botoxed,
And she smells like a loo with no flush.
And yet despite my unkindly punning,
She turns me right on and gets my motor running.

Tom Bishop (14)
Whitchurch High School, Cardiff

The Cynicism Of Winter

Winter,
Winter means changes,
Unwelcome changes that bring death to the Earth.

The cold weather destroys the fragile innocence of flowers,
Days are shorter as darkness envelops the precious light,
Poor innocent snow falls to our damned Earth so taken by sin.

The sin of Christmas runs rife as Winter reaches evil heights,
Hypocritical toilers gather to celebrate the birth of the damned,
Damned to death, only a young man.

As the season tears away at the land,
Those aged folks are taken before their time by Winter's loyal
                                                    slave of cold,
Time seems to chill in the morning while the toilers lie stiff.

Large water masses are lidded by a layer of ice,
Just waiting to crack under the first step of an innocent minor,
The ice freezes once more and the minor is trapped, damned,
                                        even younger than the man.

A little girl it seems it was who was felled by Winter's cruel hand,
As her parents weep in front of Winter's bitter enemy, Fire,
The tyrant of Winter laughs at them calling them fools in the face
                                        of their youngster's death.

As Winter closes and the sun comes out from its yearly hibernation,
People rejoice as the tyrant of Winter is forced to surrender,
Until next year when its reign of cruelty starts all over again . . .

Nathan Hickery (15)
Whitchurch High School, Cardiff

The Silence Before

Mist covers the path ahead,
No sight to see the evil leer,
Silence before, the battle soon,
Standing in line, gone are the cheers.

A slow drum beat, the only sound,
The enemy far, but near,
Darkness falls, to summon death,
Piling up, the soldiers fear.

Noticed now, the drum gets faster,
And the mist, seems too clear,
Judgement now, for the souls,
Of these men, finally here.

Owen Richards (13)
Whitchurch High School, Cardiff

Wall Of Mirrors

My past is shown from little to big
Sad to happy
Baby to child
A long film of my life shown in glass
Memories of love and tragedy in present and past
Some views are dusty some are clean
Birthdays good and bad fly through like dreams.

There's a space for my future
Shown as a dusty cloud
My adult life is not that far
So many mysteries and adventures to be revealed to me
I hope it brings good times and good memories.

Maddy O'Neill (13)
Whitchurch High School, Cardiff

The Fire!

That weird, orange type of effect,
That flutters like a wild bird.
But when it is to be touched,
Warmth and pain is given.
Its beauty can make you feel relaxed,
but can fear others.

It growls softly like a kitten's purr,
And waves its flames continuously.
It burns your thoughts and warms your feelings.
But it is dangerous too at times.

It calms the lost,
It gives light to the poor,
But it hurts the bad,
So be careful!

The fire is that weird, orange type of effect,
That flutters like a wild bird.
I like the fire,
It keeps me warm,
When I'm cold and hurt.

Its amber flames has a crimson turn,
Gold and sparkling too.
I hope you can enjoy the fire,
And it warms your feelings through!

Abbie Ognjenovic (12)
Whitchurch High School, Cardiff

Golden Summer

The golden sun floats gracefully in the sky
like an elegant ballerina dancing.
Golden sunflowers nod their heads in the breezy wind
as if talking to each other.
Busy beaches bubble in the scorching heat.
The golden grains of sand glisten
in the glare of the golden sun.

Carys Tucker (14)
Whitchurch High School, Cardiff

Emotions

I am a controlling feeling,
that makes you envy others,
I make you turn green
and wish you were them.

I am a warm feeling
that comes out of doing good.
I produce a smile that's contagious
and I can do no wrong.

I am a bad feeling
that feels like thunder striking inside you.
I make you want to scream
when I build up inside you.

I am a blue feeling
that can conjure up tears.
I make your bottom lip tremble
when I pay you a visit.

I am a worried feeling
that brings up all your anxieties and fears.
I make your heart pound
when you feel me creeping up.

Emma Keenan (12)
Whitchurch High School, Cardiff

The Kaleidoscopic Cliff

The kaleidoscopic cliff
Formed thousands of years ago
Gargantuan, iridescent, soaring
Like a tower that has no top
Like a mountain 3000 feet high,
It makes me feel diminutive,
Like a centipede people squash,
The kaleidoscopic cliff
That if you go up you never come down.

Emily Knox (11)
Whitchurch High School, Cardiff

I Am . . .

I am a delicate thing,
I am filled with colours,
I am very, very pretty,
And bees are attracted to me,
You sometimes wear me in your hair or clothes,
You give me to people on special occasions.
I am a . . .
A: Flower

I am a very bright feeling,
I give you warmth throughout the day
But go to sleep at night,
If I go away then it would be dark,
If you look at me then I will make your eyes burn.
I am . . .
A: Sunshine

I am a calm thing,
Most people love me,
I am a mammal,
I live in the sea,
I have a blowhole and fins
I am a . . .
A: Dolphin

Charlotte Camilleri (13)
Whitchurch High School, Cardiff

She Is . . .

She is a flowing summer dress,
She is a bowl of melting sorbet,
She is a warm scarf on a cold evening,
She is a bubbling bottle of pop,
She is a glowing daisy,
She is a wise owl,
She is a fizzing firework,
She is a dramatic drama lesson,
She is . . . my best friend.

Elinor Crawley (12)
Whitchurch High School, Cardiff

Winter Sonnet

Winter is an old man, wicked and mean,
Inside his tough skin there's nothing but cold,
He shows harshness of a brutal machine,
If kindness were bread, his would be all mould,
He covers the world with a blanket white,
He welcomes the robin but chases bears,
Like a rabid dog so ready to bite,
He's angry cos on his head, there's no hair,
He scares lots of birds and south they will fly,
Like a ruthless emperor ord'ring treason,
He lays down the ice so that children cry,
We'd agree that winter's the meanest season,
You say that he's frosty and bears no glee,
But he's the one that puts gifts 'neath our tree.

William Francis (13)
Whitchurch High School, Cardiff

Who Am I

I am harmless but I'm not a feather,
I can hear high-pitched noises but I'm not a dog,
I have lots of teeth but I'm not a lion,
I'm speedy but I'm not a cheetah,
I travel deep down but I'm not a mole,
I breathe air but I'm not a rabbit,
I have a blow hole but I'm not a whale,
I have two fins but I'm not a clownfish,
I have a dorsal fin but I'm not a shark,
I live in water but I'm not a fish.
Who am !?
I'm a dolphin.

Siân Crowley (12)
Whitchurch High School, Cardiff

Maths

Every minute goes by like an hour,
This lesson drains me of strength and power,
My brain is buzzing, I don't understand,
I've heard enough! My brain demands.

The teacher speaks in a continuous drone,
It makes me want to scream and moan,
The teacher speaks a load of nonsense to me,
How does that make sense? I cannot see.

I pray that the bell will ring soon,
It has seemed like it's gone on all afternoon.

Can you guess what this subject is?
Of course you can, it's *maths!*

Zoë Azzopardi (12)
Whitchurch High School, Cardiff

Sky

Fluffy white clouds wash over the endless blue colour,
They drift apart then gradually weave back together,
Forming everything from gigantic whales to tiny fish,
The sun appears from behind a fin,
The clouds scatter like children,
Its rays shine right down to the ocean bed,
Then the clouds turn grey,
Rain thunders down, splashing in every puddle,
Like teardrops falling from an eye,
The teardrops stop falling,
And the sun peeks out again from the bright blue sky.

Jo Pople (13)
Whitchurch High School, Cardiff

Beach

Here I stand
with my feet in the sand.
The waves eating at my feet.
The salt in the air,
whips at my hair.
Seaweed's clinging to my legs.
The seagulls fly
so high in the sky.
The sun shines in my eyes.

Emily Harris (13)
Whitchurch High School, Cardiff

Nine Eleven

Hoards of people sound their horns,
Beware Bin Laden America warns,
Innocent people flee their homes,
That's as far as the towers go,
They fall to the ground,
In an almighty crash,
I couldn't believe my eyes,
What has the world come to?

Alex Kerr (12)
Whitchurch High School, Cardiff

Summer

Green grass and hot afternoons,
Sun, sea and sand.
A blazing ball of fire, burning bright.
Love is in the air
No school, just fun all day long
Till the sun sets, leaving the warm
Summer nights to begin
Summer sun, gone too soon.

Alex McWhirter (13)
Whitchurch High School, Cardiff

Countryside

Countryside,
Lush, verdant, peaceful,
Full of animals, plants, strange smells and windy roads,
Bright flowers in the hedgerows waving
Crops rustling in the gentle breeze,
Farmers tending their fields,
Growing food for the nation,
Lush, verdant, busy,
Countryside.

Kathryn Powell (13)
Whitchurch High School, Cardiff

Summertime

Red, yellow, dazzling sun,
High-pitched tones that sound like fun,
No more are the short cold days,
The sun shines down with red-hot rays.
Blossoming flowers on the ground,
Birds flying high give that summery sound,
Dripping ice creams and melting flakes
These things remind me of summer breaks!

Kate Jenkins (13)
Whitchurch High School, Cardiff

I Remember

I remember when I went to Florida,
I went to all the theme parks,
Excited, happy and noisy,
Like a bomb exploding in mid-air,
Like my radio at full volume,
It made me feel happy,
Remembering my holiday in Florida,
Makes me realise how good life is.

Owain Harrison (11)
Whitchurch High School, Cardiff

Reflections And Time

I stopped,
Looked in the mirror,
Saw a reflection of me,
Time flew by quickly,
I looked in the river,
Saw a reflection of me,
Time stopped suddenly,
I looked in the sea,
Time flew by again quickly,
I looked back in the mirror,
Once more,
Time stopped time,
Didn't start again.

Hannah Jones (12)
Whitchurch High School, Cardiff

Autumn

The hundred and thousands of leaves
Red and golden brown crunching on the floor.
The bitter cold of the wind
Biting at my uncovered skin.
The bare trees
Bending and twisting with age.
The autumnal rains
Trailing down my windowpane,
Each drop rolling to the bottom.
Autumn is bare and cold
Always was, always will be.

Erin Stacey (13)
Whitchurch High School, Cardiff

The Gloomy Lane

Down the dark, gloomy lane,
All you can hear is the cry of pain,
Surrounding every corner and step,
I think I'll have to go and check.

In my head swirling round and round,
Thinking about what I'm going to find,
All these thoughts are swishing around,
I don't know what to do, I'll have to follow my mind.

One step further the sound is piercing my ears,
I'm really worried what if it's my peers,
I can't think and can hardly breath,
I hate this moment. I feel so seethed.

Lauren Morgan (12)
Whitchurch High School, Cardiff

I Miss You

It happens without warning,
Time and time again,
I try hard to forget the past,
But still remember when,
You were there to share it all,
To make it all worthwhile,
I remember the things we did,
And the fun we had,
And once again I smile.
But then reality turns back to me,
And once again, you're gone,
If only this little dream I have
Could simply just go on!

Saskia Nicolai (12)
Whitchurch High School, Cardiff

The King Of The Jungle!

Deep down in the dark, dark jungle,
The animals stop and hear a rumble,
The king of the jungle lets out a big roar,
And the animals stop and cower to the floor,
You will obey me and forever you will stay,
Trapped in the jungle, every night and day,
The animals look at each other and give a look of sadness,
How can he do this? It is madness!
We must do something whispered the animals,
We can't be kept captured like this, we're not criminals,
Off went the animals to think of a way to get out
And conjured up a magnificent way to escape,
They all crept out while the king of the jungle was asleep,
And never returned to that barbaric place,
While the animals lived their lives in grace,
And left the lion stranded in peace, all alone
And no more the animals will have to listen
To his commands or moans, or groans.

Tracey Michals (13)
Whitchurch High School, Cardiff

The Face

The face is an old crumpled piece of paper,
Green piercing eyes,
Piercing through me like spears,
Her sore, red lips crack into little pieces whenever she speaks,
Her nose as high as Mount Everest stands out
Like a sore thumb,
Her grey dirty tangled hair stands up on end,
Like soldiers standing for attention,
I just hope in years to come,
This isn't me.

Alice Barnes (14)
Whitchurch High School, Cardiff

Forgotten Girl

She was the one always held in depression's hands,
Her mind screaming at her when she ignored its commands,
Heavy lidded eyes covered the tired redness,
She hates herself more as she misses the bus,
Misery is attracted to her fragile self,
She felt really rigid, like a rag doll on a shelf,
No one acknowledged her, or knew of her being,
They didn't speak to her, or know how she was feeling,
The cuts up her arms, the tears she cried,
The things she did, the voices inside,
No friends to confide in, or family that cared,
The looks she longed for, but instead there were glares,
No one wanted to know about her,
They were stupid to forget her,
They wouldn't tell her how pretty she was inside,
Until her hopes deserted her, no faith left, her body had died.

Alexandra Dwyer (12)
Whitchurch High School, Cardiff

The Little Puppy

The little puppy
Was small, black and brown,
Energetic, fun and sweet!
It was as small as a cuddly toy,
And like a little ball of fluff,
It makes you feel happy every time you see it,
Like every time you see a rainbow,
The little puppy,
Makes me think how lucky I am to own him.

Sophie Knight (11)
Whitchurch High School, Cardiff

The Reflection Of Life

Babies are like the sun,
The dawn of life,
Children are like sunlight,
Shining bright in our life.
Teenagers are like rain clouds,
The moody, rebellious stage of life,
Adults are like windows,
The opening of life,
The elderly are like doors,
The closing of life.

Hannah Delaney (12)
Whitchurch High School, Cardiff

For The Final Time

For the final time, the whistle blew,
Over the top, the army flew,
Bullets fired one hundred a time,
Many died on the front line,
Father and son perish together,
Hand in hand to last forever,
Flanders Field where poppies grow,
Crown the heroes from years ago.

Lauren Jones (12)
Whitchurch High School, Cardiff

The Great Flats

The great flats built a couple of years ago,
Huge, mad, tall, like a tree growing into the sky,
Like a rocket going into space, it makes me feel tiny,
Like a microbus that no one notices,
The great flats,
Reminds me how small I really am.

David Thomas (11)
Whitchurch High School, Cardiff

The Great Wall

The great wall,
The great wall,
Built thousands of years ago,
Huge, mighty, soaring,
Like a wall reaching for the end,
Like a thick piece of chocolate,
It makes me feel strong,
Like a lion that no one can beat,
The great,
Reminds us how strong we are.

Rhys McCarthy (11)
Whitchurch High School, Cardiff

The Old Tree

The old tree,
Bloomed hundreds of years ago,
Thick, tall, huge,
With thousands and thousands of green leaves,
It makes me feel as small as a mouse,
But no one will notice me, only the tree,
The old tree.

Daniel Stone (11)
Whitchurch High School, Cardiff

The Old House

The old house,
Stood there for hundreds of years,
It was dark, spooky and full of cobwebs,
It was as grey as an elephant,
It makes me shiver,
Shiver like a scared dog,
The old house.

Aimee Turner (11)
Whitchurch High School, Cardiff

Colour!

Red is the burning flame of the fire,
Flickering into the wind!
Warning do not enter as the red stands tall and proud!
Autumn comes as the red paints itself onto the trees,
A beautiful colour but has so many meanings,
What does the colour red mean?

Green is the countryside,
Trees so elegant sit there for hours,
Showing their beauty off!
All different shades, light green, dark green,
So relaxing. Bushes cover the mountains,
Some so green, some sharp, some tiny,
But every little detail is beautiful!
What does the colour green mean?

Blue is the sea, cold, sharp!
The sea is cold but so elegant rippling onto the sand!
Blue makes you feel old,
But if you look before and into the colour,
You see much more!
What does the colour blue mean?

These colours have so many meanings,
But they're all so elegant.

Caroline Boyle (11)
Whitchurch High School, Cardiff

An Ancient Tomb

Where Pharaohs are buried,
Dark, large, abandoned,
Like a mountain bowing over,
Like a stairway to Heaven,
It makes me feel rested,
Like a cow in a field,
An ancient tomb,
Reminds us to enjoy life.

Gemma Lloyd (11)
Whitchurch High School, Cardiff

A Worried Soldier Worthy Of Red

A worried solider made to fight,
In a battle with dynamite,
In the mountain fog arises,
Causing many different crisis.

A glowing red sun through the fog,
Five miles further than a brownish bog,
Made to march all this way,
Can often cause many pains.

Many gallons of blood were spilt,
And many humans were killed,
A worried soldier bravely fought,
Until he pushed them back to their port.

Danger in the air,
Beginning to scare,
Many humans who just fought,
All been sent to the court.

A worried soldier just lost a fight,
In a battle of dynamite.

Adam Torjussen (11)
Whitchurch High School, Cardiff

The Great Tower

The great tower,
Built hundreds of years ago,
Huge, pointy, enormous,
Like a plant growing to the sky,
Like a rocket blasting off into space,
It makes me feel tiny,
Like a flea that no one can see,
The great tower,
Reminds us how short our lives are.

Jack Shields (11)
Whitchurch High School, Cardiff

Flowers

Flowers are pretty,
They blow in the breeze,
They make you happy,
Some make you sneeze.

They dance around
With you and I,
They think we're giants,
In the sky.

Bees buzz,
Around the flowers,
Collecting pollen,
To get more power.

But in the end,
When they die,
They shrivel away
And say, 'Bye-bye.'

Bethan Ashford (12)
Whitchurch High School, Cardiff

My Trophy

My trophy,
I won it last year,
Shiny, silver and gold,
It glistens like a star,
And stands proud like a sergeant,
It makes me feel proud,
Like a brave champion,
My trophy,
Reminds me that I'm good at something.

Zakaria Djoudi (11)
Whitchurch High School, Cardiff

De Winter Poem

De cold, de snow, de ice, de rain,
De misery again and again.
De freezin' breeze,
De slushy sleeves,
De feelin' of December.

De wind, de frost
In the mist are lost,
De cold comes in,
De heat goes out,
It's too cold to walk about.

De feelin' of December
De chilly breeze will make us sneeze,
De thinkin' of December!

Hannah Nicholas (12)
Whitchurch High School, Cardiff

Ice Cream

Ice cream is cold,
Hard to hold,
In different flavours,
It's icy, it drips,
As I eat it,
I lick my lips.

It's creamy,
So dreamy,
I could eat it every day,
Where is the ice cream van?
I hope it's on the way!

Leigh Sharman (12)
Whitchurch High School, Cardiff

Hurricanes!

H urry, hurry, quick, quick,
U p the stair, snip, snip,
R un, run, doesn't matter,
R uining people, splatter, splatter,
I ris, Bonnie,
C harlie too,
A ngry winds,
N ever true,
E verlasting until they die.

    Hurricanes flying through the sky!

Laura Brewer (12)
Whitchurch High School, Cardiff

Homework

H omework is loving
O hh no not more
M ove, move, move
E very day
W ork, work, work, no time to play
O ral assignment and written ASs
R eading and writing, no time to play
K nowledge is something that adults have.

Aneurin Campbell (11)
Whitchurch High School, Cardiff

I Love Love!

L ight and happiness is suddenly in your life,
O ver the moon with joy and pride,
V ery happy you make me my dear,
E very day, every month, every year!
   I love love!

Amy Deering (11)
Whitchurch High School, Cardiff

The Book

The book,
Filled with years of writing,
Funny, dramatic, mysterious,
Like a key to another,
Like a world of literacy,
Makes you feel entranced,
Like you're controlled by a hypnotist,
The book,
Gives us back our imagination.

Bryn William Rogers (11)
Whitchurch High School, Cardiff

The Great Olympics

The great Olympics,
Invented hundreds of years ago,
Mighty, great, famous,
Like a race of the gods,
Like a united world,
It makes me feel like a champion,
The great Olympics,
Reminds me of how great sport is.

Alun Cadogan (11)
Whitchurch High School, Cardiff

The Great Television

The great television set
Built by Logie Baird,
Small, big, medium televisions,
Like an electrical box,
It makes me feel tiny,
Like a person that has no importance,
The great television set
Reminds me of how much technology we have.

Liam Venus (11)
Whitchurch High School, Cardiff

My Childhood

I don't remember much about my childhood,
It all seems a blur,
Apart from the things that made me angry like
My teddy's matted fur.

I remember the smell of my mum making bread for my lunch,
As is sat by the fire thinking, *I'm hungry* . . .
Is it time for brunch?

I used to love my bright green dummy,
And the taste of chocolate milk, yummy, yummy, yummy!

As autumn went and winter came,
I remember me and my wellies dancing in the rain.

Then I'd go to sleep at night,
And dream sweet dreams,
As my mum would sing to me,
And smile sweetly, looking down at me.

Jessica Hall (14)
Whitchurch High School, Cardiff

Mount Everest

Mount Everest,
Thousands and thousands,
Metres high,
Gigantic, mighty, flying,
Like a finger pointing at Heaven,
Like a white sheet spread over a hill,
It makes me feel like I am floating,
Like an eagle floating in the sky,
Mount Everest,
Makes me feel so small.

Lily Cleall-Harding (11)
Whitchurch High School, Cardiff

Sunshine

Pink
Pink roses and blossoms,
Swaying from side to side.

Purple
Purple is made up from blue and yellow
It always makes me happy.

Yellow
Yellow is happy and warm,
Yellow reminds me of a happy smiling face.

Red
Red is deep and bloody, dark and lost,
On a battlefield full of dead bodies.

Diva Deane (11)
Whitchurch High School, Cardiff

Gargantuan Tree

The gargantuan tree,
Crisp, green leaves,
Vast, strong, ancient,
Like a tower growing through the clouds,
As wide as the universe,
Making me feel as if it is full of wisdom,
Like a wise old man,
The gargantuan tree,
Reminding me how long the universe has existed.

Alexandra Bond (11)
Whitchurch High School, Cardiff

Everybody

E verybody is different,
V ery, very different,
E verybody is different,
R arely the same,
Y ou and me are different,
B ut everybody's got a name,
O nly some people don't have a name,
D on't you have a name?
Y ou and me are different.

Krystal Mills (11)
Whitchurch High School, Cardiff

The Panda Bear

A giant panda,
Endangered all over the world,
Gigantic, cuddly, warm,
Like a huge dinosaur cuddling the world,
Like a teddy bear so gentle and fuzzy,
He makes me feel safe,
Like toast with runny butter,
A giant panda,
Reminds me of how precious wildlife is.

Jessica Bishop (11)
Whitchurch High School, Cardiff

I Don't Know

In a world of Versace, Armarni and Gucci,
£10,000 dresses and £5,000 shoes,
Diet pills and the Atkins,
Britney Spears and Madonna,
Why are people dying of diseases that can be cured?
Why are people starving?
Why are children scared to go home?

Gemma Fitzgibbon (13)
Whitchurch High School, Cardiff

I Remember

I remember my nightie,
Made from silk,
Now it's stained,
By chocolate milk.

I can remember playing games,
Sitting by the fire next to nice, warm flames.

I watched 'Rosie and Jim',
I fought over teddies
Till they ripped limb from limb.

I remember falling downstairs,
Making dens, hanging sheets from chairs.

Samantha Boothroyd (14)
Whitchurch High School, Cardiff

The Colour Red

Red
Red is the feeling of fire when you get home,
Red is the sun beaming on us on a hot summer's day,
Red is the taste of ripe strawberries freshly picked,
Red is the sound of hearts on February 14th,
Red is the smell of freshly made cranberry juice,
Red is the colour of anger,
Red is the colour of everyone's favourite sweet,
Red is the colour of the topping of my pizza,
Red shows us the dangers on the road,
Red is the colour of the treats we all love.

Joanne Bloom (11)
Whitchurch High School, Cardiff

The Lonely House

The lonely house,
Still on its own,
Standing proud and tall.

People walked by,
Thinking it don't
Make sense at all,
It was creepy and still.

With no movement no more!
So that's the story of the
Lonely house.

Kelly Shaw (11)
Whitchurch High School, Cardiff

Red Is . . .

Red is a confident colour,
It stands for danger,
It stands for stop,
It is the colour of fire,
It is the colour of blood.

A worried soldier standing,
Or an empty battlefield,
To see that everywhere is red,
The red devil who accidentally
Killed the angel.

Cameron Stacey (11)
Whitchurch High School, Cardiff

One Day . . .

Nobody's ever cared about me in
    the way I always desired,
And now I'm ready to give up,
    to be honest I'm getting too tired,
To chase around and be all nice,
    and pretend I'm something I'm not
Trying to win appreciation
    from those who just haven't got
Any understanding of who I am,
    why I smile, or why I cry,
But more importantly why I'm left to think
    to myself, why me? Why?
Did I do something I don't know about,
    to deserve such uncertainty today?
Or am I paying a debt for something?
    Are you showing me the way?
The you I speak of exists,
    in the darkness of my heart,
You live and sacrifice so many things,
    just to learn the art,
Of trust, love and honesty
    things I need to learn to convey,
To ensure my sanity in my life
    and survive from day to day.

Kayley Davies-Richards (17)
Ysgol Gyfun Bro Myrddin, Carmarthenshire

The Secret

You don't know it
You don't know the secret
And I shall tell it to no one
To no one
Because I promised.

People want to know my secret
It's why they brought me here
It's why they put me in this place
It's why they put me in this room.

And it's why they watch me
Yes, they watch me.
They think I don't know
But I do.
I know they watch me
But I shan't tell them
I'll tell no one
Because I promised.

They say that the secret is naughty,
They say that I'm naughty not to tell it
But to break a promise is naughty,
And I promised.

I promised him I'd never tell.

It's our little secret.

Have you guessed the secret?
I don't mind if you have,
I trust you,
But promise me you'll never tell it,
Promise me,
Promise
Tell no one,
Tell no one the secret!

Hannah Jones (17)
Ysgol Gyfun Bro Myrddin, Carmarthenshire